SELF-INFLICTED WOUNDS: RUSSIA'S FAILED CHECHEN AND NORTH CAUCASUS POLICY

The fall of the Berlin Wall in October 1989[1] ushered a period of internal strife and uncertainty into the Soviet Union (USSR). As Western ideals and products flowed in through this rent in communism, Moscow's leadership fractured between communist party hard-liners resisting reform, Mikhail Gorbachev, who wanted to reform but retain the communist system, and Boris Yeltsin, who advocated for state independence and democracy.

The cumbersome and lethargic communist central planning system clashed with Gorbachev's attempts at market reform, and the resultant economic crises caused the system to collapse under its own weight, leading to the dissolution of the Soviet Union on December 31, 1991.[2] Boris Yeltsin emerged out of the ashes of the USSR, leading a newly independent Russia. Several republics of the Soviet Union took advantage of this chaos and Yeltsin's advocacy of democracy to declare their independence, starting with the Baltic States, then the Ukraine and Georgia, and finally Chechnya (for further background on the dissolution of the Soviet Union, see endnote[3]).

Chechnya declared its independence from the USSR in November 1991.[4] Unlike the peripheral republics that sought independence however, Chechnya was an integral part of Russia, and Chechen independence threatened Russia's territorial integrity.[5] Boris Yeltsin had to draw the line at this threat, and the fledgling Russian government therefore declared Chechnya's independence unconstitutional, but was able to do little else while Russia focused on its economic woes from 1991-1993.[6]

By 1994, public order in Chechnya had eroded[7] and was threatening Chechnya's substantial ethnic Russian population.[8] Also at risk was the important oil industry in Chechnya, including refineries in the capital city of Grozny, and pipelines running through the republic from the Caspian to the Black Seas.[9] Chechen secession posed the risk of a domino effect among other republics seeking their own independence.[10]

Yeltsin therefore sent Russian military forces into Chechnya in a vicious military operation lasting from 1994-1996,[11] in order to preserve the integrity of the Russian Federation.[12] Hostilities between Russian forces and Chechen rebels were repeated by President Putin in a 1999-2009 war that lay waste to the Chechen capital city of Grozny,[13] caused the displacement of approximately 200,000 refugees,[14] and killed an estimated 100,000 people, among them both combatants and non-combatants.[15]

The Russian government's harsh methods during both wars have resulted in continued attacks by Chechen rebels against Russian and pro-Moscow Chechen forces, and have caused instability in Chechnya.[16] The United Nations and human rights organizations have repeatedly condemned the ruthless methods used against the Chechen people by Russian military and security forces,[17] but the Russian government has rebuffed the resolutions and allegations.[18] The conflicts have also caused spillover violence in the North Caucasus,[19] and have resulted in reprisal attacks against Russian targets.[20] The Kremlin's response has been limited predominantly to the use of force and population control measures against its Caucasian population.

Russia's reliance on military force and the aggressive application of population control measures against its Caucasian population, while ignoring other options for conflict resolution, has ensured continued discord in the North Caucasus, jeopardizing the flow of Russian energy in the Caspian basin, and endangers future Federation stability and security.

Approach

This paper surveys the recent history and nature of Russian combat operations against Chechen separatists, describes attacks against the Russian Federation, and addresses the widening insurgency in the North Caucasus resulting from those operations. Such a survey enables a comparison and evaluation of the effectiveness of Russia's response to such incidents at a policy and an operational level, and explores ways to improve that response (for an overview of events and key figures referred to in this paper, see endnote[21]).

The Russian government has endured a series of attacks against its interests within the Russian Federation as a result of the conflicts in Chechnya, and responded predominantly with the use of force. This paper describes why this limited method has failed, and recommends ways in which Russia can more effectively develop an approach to mitigate future incidents and to stabilize Chechnya and the North Caucasus region.

Russia wants stability and security in the North Caucasus for primarily economic reasons, but also to mitigate attacks against its interests within the Russian Federation.[22] The North Caucasus region is important to Russia because it lies between the Caspian and Black Seas and is a nexus of energy flow for oil and gas pipelines.[23] Moving energy through this region from Caspian Sea terminals is the most direct route to markets in Mediterranean Europe,[24] and avoids the need to build and maintain pipelines to divert energy around areas experiencing insurgent conflict.[25]

Additionally, Russia won the right to host the 2014 Winter Olympics in Sochi, which is a city in the Krasnodar Territory of Russia.[26] Sochi is a resort area on the Black Sea coast, which nestles against the North Caucasus mountain range.[27] Sochi lies perilously close to areas with ongoing insurgent conflict,[28] and this proximity presents a tempting target to rebel leadership.[29]

The people of the North Caucasus also want stability and security in the region.[30,31] The widening insurgency is a symptom of the underlying causes of the conflict that have caused nearly two decades of strife in the North Caucasus territories. Unemployment in the region hovers between 50-75%.[32] Nearly 200,000 non-combatants fled the fighting in Chechnya to nearby Ingushetia and many have yet to be resettled.[33] Security concerns have prevented most non-governmental organizations from assisting the refugees, which has exacerbated the poor living conditions in the camps.[34] The ongoing instability and violence in the region has increased unemployment, and created fertile ground for insurgent recruitment.[35]

After two wars and hundreds of thousands of casualties among both combatants and non-combatants, peace in the region is no closer than when the conflict began in 1994.[36] Insurgent attacks continue against Russian and pro-Moscow targets in Chechnya, and have touched nearly every republic and territory of the North Caucasus.[37] The insurgency is spreading throughout the North Caucasus, and attacks emanating from the region continue against targets in Moscow, the capital of Russia.[38] It is imperative for the Kremlin leadership to find incentives that will pull the insurgents away from fighting and into rebuilding their infrastructure and homes, as well as providing employment for insurgent fighters and those unemployed.

4

Russia must use an array of domestic as well as international aid to rebuild infrastructure and employ Chechens and North Caucasians, and to restore the efficient flow of energy (oil and gas) from the Caspian to the Black Sea, which runs through Chechnya and the North Caucasus.[39] The existing pipelines that transit the region have been illegally tapped and attacked repeatedly.[40] Grozny's refineries were also destroyed during the fighting,[41] which has resulted in the restriction of petroleum throughput.[42] The stability and restoration of this energy conduit is vital to the economic future of Russia.[43]

Such measures would be a win-win for Russia and the residents of the North Caucasus, if Russia employs locals to do the construction and rebuilding. The insurgents would have an incentive to stop fighting, and earned income would go into the hands of the local population, which would help energize the region's economies. A self-policing mechanism is then provided for former insurgents, since new jobs encourage economic growth, and will deter future attacks on the infrastructure that employs them.

Background

The reasons for the current conditions in the North Caucasus are diverse and complex, but began with Russia's first military intervention into Chechnya in 1994.[44] The heavy-handed tactics employed by Russian forces in that conflict led to widespread lawlessness in Chechnya and the spillover of violence into the surrounding region, [45] resulting in a second Chechen war in 1999.[46] The brutality and utter devastation visited upon Chechnya by Russian forces during the second war brought reprisal attacks into Russia with increasing regularity and severity,[47] and have led to a widening and ongoing insurgency among the Muslim population of the North Caucasus.[48]

<u>Chechnya</u>

Chechnya is a 4,750 square mile, mostly Muslim republic in the North Caucasus region of Russia with a population of about 1.2 million (2008 estimate).[49] The region has always been contentious. Russian czars conquered the area in the 19th century, but a low-level insurgency continued, led by the Muslim leader Shamil until his capture in 1859.[50] In 1944 Joseph Stalin forcibly deported the entire Chechen population to Kazakhstan for fear that they would collude with the advancing Germans. In 1957 Soviet leader Nikita Khrushchev permitted the surviving exiles to return to their homeland.[51]

<u>The First Chechen War</u>

In August 1991, due to the breakup of the Soviet Union and rapid declarations of independence by many former Soviet republics, former Soviet Air Force General and Chechen politician, Dzhokhar Dudayev, carried out a successful coup d'état against the communist Chechen government, and was elected Chechen president in October 1991.[52] In November 1991, Dudayev declared Chechen independence from Russia.[53] This attempt to break away prompted the December 1994, Russian invasion of Chechnya by Russian President Boris Yeltsin and his Prime Minister, Vladimir Putin. After fierce fighting, Russian forces succeeded in occupying all of the Chechen republic's urban areas, but could not defeat the rebels in the mountainous south.[54]

During the fighting and the rebel insurgency that followed, an estimated 60,000-100,000 people died, and more than 200,000 were wounded.[55] In April 1996, Dudayev was killed by a Russian missile attack that targeted his satellite phone, and Zemlikhan Yandarbiyev succeeded him.[56] President Yeltsin and Yandarbiyev signed a truce that ended the war in August 1996, and the Chechen rebels re-took Grozny.[57] Following the rebel reoccupation of the city, President Yeltsin's security chief General Alexander Lebed and the Chechen rebel chief of staff Aslan Maskhadov, who was a former Soviet artillery officer, signed a provisional treaty known as the Khasavyurt Peace Accords.[58] The treaty provided for a cease-fire under which Russian troops withdrew from Chechnya, and any discussions of future Chechen independence were to be shelved for a period of five years.[59]

Russian Antiterrorism Law

In the 1990's, according to Viktor Petrischev of the Russian State Duma (the lower house of the Russian National Parliament[60]), Russia experienced an increase in social unrest and disorder, "crime, extremism, and terrorism,"[61] as a result of the Russian governments policies of democratic reform.[62] Petrischev claimed that these conditions were enabled by, "economic decline, deterioration of interethnic relations, growth of separatism, and loss of the values that formerly bound the society together, such as civic duty, patriotism, and internationalism."[63]

Petrischev further claimed that politicians vying for power unwittingly exacerbated the situation by holding unsanctioned political gatherings that stirred their followers to demand change leading to demonstrations and riots.[64] The ensuing disorder nearly led to the collapse of the Russian state.[65] Boris Yeltsin unwittingly exacerbated the problem while cultivating democratic reform amongst the ashes of the USSR by encouraging the republics of the Soviet Union "to take as much sovereignty as they can possibly swallow."[66] This exhortation resulted in a flood of independence movements, some permitted by the Russian state (as in the Ukraine),[67] and some not (as in Tatarstan and Chechnya).[68] In the case of Chechnya, the thirst for independence led to armed conflict.

The criminality and armed conflict that occurred as a result of the Russian governments policies of democratic reform demonstrated the need for a national policy on counterterrorism,[69] and therefore in March 1996, Russian President Boris Yeltsin directed the creation of an antiterrorism law,[70] and on 25 July 1998 he signed the law into effect.[71] Part of the law describes "the organization of an illegal armed formation" as a terrorist act.[72] This is significant for Chechnya because the Kremlin calls armed rebels or separatists, "illegal armed formations," and this verbiage has allowed Russia to define Chechen rebels as terrorists as opposed to persons vying for independence.[73]

The law also created negative implications for civil liberties, allowing Russian authorities to institute harsh population control measures during counterterrorist operations.[74] Additionally, the media, or citizens of the Russian Federation, are prevented from covering events or publishing articles that are perceived to favor rebels or suggest that the rebels are conducting an insurgency versus terrorist activities.[75]

Russian newspapers suggesting a political settlement to the Chechen conflict received stern warnings from Russian authorities.[76] The Russian Ministry of Press also admonished prominent Russian newspapers for interviewing Chechen leaders, including the Moscow newspaper Kommersant for interviewing the former President of Chechnya, Aslan Maskhadov on February 7, 2005.[77]

Post Conflict, 1997-1999

In January 1997, following the relative peace in Chechnya that accompanied the Khasavyurt Peace Accords ending the first Chechen war, rebel military commander Aslan Maskhadov won presidential elections in Chechnya, and his government was recognized by Russian President Boris Yeltsin later that year.[78] Maskhadov, though a Muslim, was a moderate whose goal was Chechen independence.[79] Maskhadov favored direct negotiations with Moscow to secure independence or a high degree of autonomy from the Russian government.[80]

From May 1997 through early 1999, a high degree of lawlessness developed in Chechnya, including a growing number of kidnappings, among them the Russian presidential representative to Chechnya.[81] President Maskhadov became alarmed enough at the lawlessness to declare a state of emergency in June 1998.[82] Despite the increased security, in March 1999, Moscow's envoy to Chechnya was kidnapped from the Grozny airport, and his body was later found in March 2000.[83] These events caused a significant rift between the Chechen rebel leaders. In early 1999 a group of rebel commanders, including Shamil Basayev and the foreign-born rebel leader Habib Aburrahman Khattab announced the formation of a parallel government in Chechnya governed by Shariah law, and called for Maskhadov to step down as president.[84]

Prelude to the Second Chechen War: The Apartment Bombings

In September 1999 four apartment bombings rocked Russia, killing over 200 people and wounding hundreds more.[85] A fifth bomb was discovered in the basement of an apartment building and defused.[86] Theories on the purpose, and accusations as to those responsible have ranged from Chechen rebels to the FSB (the Russian Federal Security Service, formerly the KGB).[87] Several things are certain: the bombings were used in part to justify a second invasion of Chechnya, and evidence of Chechen guilt was never proven.[88] Members of the government immediately blamed the Chechens, and thus began a campaign of repression against Chechens and Caucasians throughout Russia.[89]

The bomb that was defused was found on the night of September 22, 1999, to the south of Moscow in Ryazan, Russia.[90] Authorities discovered the explosive device in the basement of a building filled with sleeping residents after being alerted to a suspicious car by alert residents.[91] Local police reported that the bomb consisted of several bags of explosives labeled as sugar.[92] The Federal Security Service of the Russian Federation (the FSB, formerly the KGB) chief announced later that his agents had planted the device themselves to test the alertness of the populace.[93]

The FSB stated that the bags actually contained sugar; however, Andrei Stolyarov, producer of the "Independent Investigations" television program produced a show that stated that most residents in Ryazan believed that the bomb was real.[94] A reporter from "Novaya Gazeta," an independent Moscow newspaper, interviewed the explosives expert who tested the white powder found in the bags; the tests proved that the substance was hexogen, which is the same kind of explosive used in the other apartment blasts.[95] The same expert also stated the initiator was genuine.[96] Further, several soldiers interviewed at a base near Ryazan who had been guarding sacks labeled as sugar became suspicious after attempting to use a bit of the substance to sweeten their tea, and after tasting the material took a sample to their commander who identified the substance as hexogen.[97]

Several political opponents of then acting President Putin tried to raise the issue just days before Presidential elections.[98] Gennady Zyuganov felt there was evidence to suggest that the bombings were conducted to bolster the government's actions in Chechnya.[99] Aside from Zyuganov, another presidential contender, Grigory Yavlinsky called for a parliamentary resolution to investigate.[100] However, Putin supporters who voted against it defeated the resolution.[101]

Russian media magnate Boris Berezovsky also stated he believed members of the Russian government coordinated the bombings to facilitate Russia's re-invasion of Chechnya.[102] Berezovsky premiered a portion of a French documentary at a news conference in London, England that showed dated photos which he said proves the detonator was real.[103] A former FSB explosives expert supported Berezovsky's claim by stating that prior to the explosions the FSB bought large amounts of Hexogen.[104] After Berezovsky made his allegations the director of the FSB Nikolai Patrushev asserted he had evidence that showed Berezovsky was providing financial support to leaders of the Chechen rebels.[105] Berezovsky has never been charged in connection with these claims.[106]

Russian authorities blamed Chechen rebels for the bombings and the resulting climate of anxiety and panic garnered popular support for the Russian government's decision to re-invade the separatist state.[107] Few questioned Putin and those that did were silenced by counter-accusations or intimidation, as was done with Berezovsky.[108]

Putin capitalized on these attacks to win the presidential elections of 2000.[109] His tough rhetoric resonated with Russians.[110] Putin promised to mobilize all necessary forces to defeat the rebels, despite the lack of evidence that the Chechens were responsible.[111] The Chechen rebels denied the claims.[112] Many continue to suspect the FSB but the suspicions remain unsubstantiated.[113] President Putin dismissed the accusations, claiming "There is nobody in the Russian special services capable of committing such a crime against our people."[114] Regardless, a Russian minority continues to harbor skepticism in relation to the government's role.

In March 2001 the Dagestani Supreme Court gave two Dagestani men life sentences for the Buinaksk, Dagestan bombing, while four other Dagestanis were convicted of acting as accomplices and received lesser sentences.[115] All of the men pled not guilty.[116] In July 2001 five men went on trial in the Stavropol territory for complicity in the Moscow bombings.[117] They were accused of delivering the explosives in sugar sacks to Moscow from the Karacheyevo-Cherkessia region, which is located in the North Caucasus.[118] In December 2001, the Stavropol territorial court sentenced the men to prison terms ranging from nine to fifteen years.[119]

Russian President Boris Yeltsin and Prime Minister Vladimir Putin ordered heightened security throughout the country following the bombings in September 1999, and police presence tripled in Moscow.[120] Moscow Mayor Yuri Lushkov directed police to conduct searches of "every market, every shop, every warehouse, and every entrance to a block of flats and every basement in the city."[121] Putin appealed to citizens to be vigilant and protect themselves.[122] This sudden activity was part of "Operation Whirlwind", a nationwide operation launched by the police and FSB in order to find those responsible for the apartment bombings and prevent further attacks.[123]

Vladimir Zubkov, Deputy Director of the Ministry of the Interior Press Service said, as a result of Operation Whirlwind we found many people without proper registration, and many others with registrations who couldn't satisfactorily explain their business in Moscow."[124] Zubkov also stated, "So far we haven't deported anyone, but all the machinery is in place to start deportations if the mayor orders it."[125]

Svetlana Alieva, a political scientist working with the Confederation of Repressed Peoples, a public organization which researches Soviet-era crimes against humanity said, "Chechens in Moscow today are like Jews in Nazi Germany."[126] The current atmosphere in Moscow is charged with fear and apprehension, very reminiscent of the communist past.[127] Not only Chechens but all dark people from the Caucasus are afraid to go into the streets, because they can be subject to summary arrest and beatings."[128]

Human rights organizations claimed that police in Moscow were targeting Chechens and other Caucasians.[129] Police checked all vehicles entering and departing Moscow,[130] and were empowered to stop anyone to check their identification; those without proper documents were subject to arrest.[131] Moscow visitors had to register with the police every 45 days; neglecting to do so could result in deportation or arrest.[132]

In September 1999, Moscow police detained more than 20,000 people, most of Caucasian descent.[133] Human rights groups reported widespread abuses of detainees.[134] Russian landlords evicted Chechens and confiscated their property. A Youth Institute poll in August 1999 showed that 54 percent of Moscow's residents, "strongly dislike" Caucasians.[135]

The Second Chechen War

In August and again in September 1999, Chechen militants led by Shamil Basayev invaded Dagestan to link up with Dagestani militants whose aim was to topple the existing Dagestan government.[136] During this time the apartment bombings took place in Russia killing more than 200 people.[137] The Russian government blamed Chechen rebels for the bombings.[138] From September 19-22, 1999, Russian Federal troops moved to and massed on the Dagestani-Chechen border.[139] Putin vowed to destroy all terrorists in Chechnya.[140]

On the 29th of September Russia's Foreign Minister, Igor Ivanov, announced that the Russian government was willing to talk with the Chechen government if they extradited Basayev.[141] At that point however, it was unclear what, if any control that President Maskhadov had over Shamil Basayev.[142] Maskhadov denounced Basayev's incursion into Dagestan, but made no apparent effort to rein in Basayev or assist in his capture.[143] The Russian government then announced it no longer recognized the Chechen government of President Aslan Maskhadov (Maskhadov then became the leader of the Chechen rebels), and on September 30, 1999, Russian forces began ground combat operations in Chechnya.[144] By the first week of October 1999, Russian forces occupied a third of Chechnya and had advanced to the outskirts of Grozny.[145]

Russia's official reason for breaking the 1996 cease-fire and reinvading Chechnya was to interdict the Islamic insurgents who had launched the separatist insurrection in neighboring Dagestan.[146] The attack also served as a reprisal for the apartment bombings that Putin blamed on the Chechen rebels.[147] The Kremlin had political and economic reasons as well; Chechnya and the North Caucasus region are strategically important to Russia.[148]

Chechnya is wedged between the Black and Caspian Seas, and the region is the conduit for lucrative Caspian Sea oil pipelines.[149] The main source of the Chechen economy before the 1994-1996 war had been petroleum, with drilling taking place to the east of Grozny, oil refining in Grozny, and a major oil pipeline running east to west between the Caspian and Black Seas.[150] Natural gas is also abundant in Chechnya and runs in pipelines towards the west.[151] The region also provides Russia access to the Black and Caspian seas for trade.[152] Approximately one million ethnic Russians live in the Caucasus region,[153] and Russia harbored fears of a domino effect of republics attempting to break away if Chechnya succeeded in gaining its independence.[154]

The 1994-1996 war saw atrocities committed by both sides, on both combatants and civilians.[155] Poorly paid Russian soldiers and officers regularly sold confiscated weapons to rebels, or traded them for vodka.[156] Both sides detained combatants and non-combatants and sold them back for a fee.[157] There is a great deal of bad blood from the first war, and the brutal conduct of the second war has only furthered the anger.

Russian "zachistki," or clearing operations have received harsh criticisms from the international community, as large numbers of detainees have disappeared while in custody.[158] The Chechen population despises the Russian forces for their harsh tactics.[159] The first war devastated the region, destroying towns and ruining infrastructure.[160] The most recent war cut off power and heat to most towns and villages and led more than 200,000 people to flee to refugee camps in neighboring Ingushetia.[161] Humanitarian groups and the Chechen government complained that Russian forces cut off all humanitarian corridors leading out of Chechnya, which prevented aid from flowing in, and refugees flowing out.[162]

By February 2000, Russian forces were in control of Grozny, which was by then mostly in ruin.[163] In June 2000, Chechen fighters carried out suicide attacks on Russian forces for the first time.[164] In May 2000, after Russian forces had secured Grozny, President Putin appointed Akhmed Kadyrov, a Chechen, to serve as an interim leader until the country was stable enough for elections.[165]

In March 2003, despite continued combat, a referendum was held in Chechnya to determine if the Chechen population was in favor of the adoption of a new constitution.[166] The constitution stated, in part, that Chechnya was to remain within the Russian Federation.[167] The referendum carried, but not without sharp criticisms by the rebels, human rights groups, non-governmental organizations (NGO's) and the Chechen people themselves.[168]

Thirty Russian non-governmental organizations (NGO's) petitioned President Putin to call off the referendum, reminding him that Chechnya already had a constitution, having been adopted after Chechnya declared independence in 1992, and recognized by Russia after Aslan Maskhadov was elected Chechen President in 1997.[169] The Organization for Security and Cooperation in Europe (OSCE) refused to send observers.[170] Russian government and pro-Moscow Chechen appointees wrote the document without rebel participation and with their grievances being ignored.[171] Additionally, 38,000 Russian servicemen stationed in Chechnya were permitted to vote, which is akin to having coalition forces serving in Afghanistan vote on the adoption of a constitution for that country.[172] Rebel leaders stated that the referendum was unacceptable and called for negotiations.[173]

In October 2003, President Putin's interim leader of Chechnya, Akhmad Kadyrov, was elected Chechen President by a huge margin with turnout said to be as high as 81%.[174] Human rights groups however, dismissed the election as illegitimate and the OSCE again did not send observers.[175] Rebel forces boycotted the election as well.[176] Rebel leader Aslan Maskhadov, himself the democratically elected president of Chechnya until the 1999 Russian invasion, stated that the proceedings would not stop their struggle for independence.[177] Maskhadov said that the election was a "criminal action by an occupation force."[178] President Putin however, described the election as part of a plan to stabilize Chechnya, along with the recent adoption of a constitution, and said that these actions would give Chechnya "autonomy in the broadest sense of the word."[179]

In May 2004, President Kadyrov was killed in a bombing at Grozny's Dinamo stadium during a WWII victory parade along with dozens of others.[180] The bomb was reportedly located near the VIP section where Kadyrov was seated.[181] An investigation revealed that the explosive device had been built into the concrete of the VIP seating area during renovations.[182]

Kadyrov had no lack of enemies in Chechnya.[183] He was a rebel leader during the first Chechen war, calling for jihad against Russian forces, but denounced the insurgency in 1999 and sided with Moscow.[184] This action earned him the position of interim leader of Chechnya as designated by President Putin.[185] Aslan Maskhadov and other Chechen rebels considered him a traitor and had tried to kill him numerous times before the Dinamo stadium bombing.[186] Following Kadyrov's death, President Putin appointed Sergei Abramov, Chechnya's Prime Minister, as acting president until elections could take place.[187]

Between the death of Kadyrov in 2004 and the announced cessation of counter-terrorism operations in Chechnya in April 2009, many political positions changed. In August 2004, Alu Alkhanov, former Chechen Interior Minister and Russian-backed candidate, won Chechen elections for the Presidency.[188] In March 2006, Ramzan Kadyrov, son of former President Akhmad Kadyrov assumed the position of Chechen Prime Minister, replacing Sergei Abramov.[189] In March 2007, President Alu Alkhanov accepted a position in the Russian government, and Ramzan Kadyrov became Chechen President, a position that he still holds.[190]

During the same period there were also changes in rebel leadership. The foreign-born rebel commander Khattab died in April 2002, after receiving a poisoned letter surreptitiously delivered by the Russian Security Service.[191] In February 2005, rebel leader and democratically elected Chechen President Aslan Maskhadov reached out to Moscow to try and establish peace talks after calling for a cease-fire.[192] Chechen President Alu Alkhanov rejected Maskhadov's proposal and instead suggested that he should turn himself in.[193] The following month, in March 2005, Russian Special Forces killed Maskhadov.[194] In June 2006, one of the last remaining Chechen rebel leaders, Abdul Saydullayev was killed in combat.[195] Saydullayev was succeeded by Doku Umarov, who is currently the most prominent rebel leader in Chechnya.[196] In July 2006, Russian forces in Ingushetia killed Shamil Basayev.[197]

Routine rebel attacks against Russian and pro-Moscow Chechen forces persist in Chechnya and areas surrounding it, and attacks continue on Russian and Chechen governmental forces to the present.[198] These tactics will likely endure, and Russian forces will continue to find that strictly military force will not prevail. Nevertheless, in April 2009, President Putin declared that counterterrorism operations had ended in Chechnya, and Russian conventional forces began a phased withdrawal.[199] The bulk of security operations were transitioned to the republics military, militia, and police forces, with the support of Russian Special Forces and Russian special anti-terrorism police and military forces.[200]

Attacks in Russia

The Russian heartland has not been spared violence from Chechnya and the North Caucasus. Since the 1999 apartment bombings[201] until present, there have been a series of high profile attacks against Russian targets attributed to insurgents from the

North Caucasus. The majority of those attacks have occurred in Moscow, the Russian capital.

Moscow Pushkinskaya Metro Bombing. During evening rush hour on August 8, 2000, a bomb exploded in the Pushkinskaya Metro Station in the center of Moscow, killing 13 people and injuring 118.[202] According to police reports and the accounts of witnesses, two men, one of whom appeared to be of Caucasian descent, left several bags near a currency exchange kiosk and departed the underpass.[203] Minutes later the bag exploded, sending shrapnel from screws packed into the explosive throughout the surrounding kiosks and underpass.[204] Despite intensive investigations, no one has been detained or charged in connection with the attack, and it is not known if the attack was the result of a terrorist attack, organized crime, or had other motives.[205]

Supporters of Vladimir Zhirinovsky, leader of the Liberal Democratic Party of Russia, displayed a banner near the Kremlin that read, "A good Chechen is a dead Chechen."[206] Moscow Mayor Yuri Luzhkov labeled the explosion a terrorist act, and President Putin convened an emergency meeting of his officials and expressed condolences to the public for the injured.[207] Russian Security Council Secretary Sergei Ivanov called for public vigilance, and police in the city were put on full alert.[208]

Moscow Hostage Crisis. On October 23, 2002, a group of 41 Chechen rebels took more than 800 people hostage at Moscow's Dubrovka theater.[209] The hostage takers configured the building to detonate with explosives, including bombs attached to female rebels.[210] Movsar Barayev, a relative of a senior Chechen rebel, led the group.[211] The Chechens demanded an immediate end to the Chechen war, the withdrawal of

Russian forces from the country, and negotiations with Chechen rebel leader Aslan Maskhadov.[212] They threatened to execute hostages if their demands were not met.[213]

After hearing shots fired on Saturday morning, Russian Special Forces infused the building with an opiate that rendered most of the occupant's unconscious.[214] It was later determined that a young Russian boy had become upset, threw a can and began running in an aisle.[215] The hostage takers fired on the boy but missed, instead striking two hostages in their seats.[216] Thirty minutes after deploying the gas the Special Forces assaulted the building, killing the hostage takers.[217] Some of the rebels that had not been affected by the gas fought back and were killed, while others who had been overcome were shot where they were found.[218]

The hostages were removed from the building, but immediate medical care and sufficient transportation means to hospitals was not available.[219] As a result 129 hostages died, after being overcome by the gas.[220] Complicating the medical issue was the fact that the type of gas used was not released for reasons of secrecy; as a result doctors waited for hours before learning the drug used.[221] Had they known of the drug during the raid, they could have had enough antidotes on hand to counter its effects.[222]

The immediate effect of the crisis was backlash against Moscow's Chechen, Dagestani, Ingush, and other Caucasian ethnicities in Russia's capital.[223] Apartments were searched, warrants were issued for the arrest of Chechens, and searches and detentions were conducted.[224] A week after the siege began President Putin announced a U.S. style war on terrorism.[225] Putin stated that, "Russia will never deal with terrorists, and will not submit to blackmail."[226] He labeled Chechen separatist leader Aslan Maskhadov a terrorist, and claimed that he would only discuss unconditional surrender as regards operations in Chechnya.[227] A poll conducted by the All-Russian Center for the Study of Public Opinion (VTsIOM), showed that 85% of respondents supported Putin's position.[228]

Moscow Avtozavodskaya / Paveletskaya Metro Bombing. On the morning of February 6, 2004, an explosion took place on a Moscow subway car between the Avtozavodskaya and Paveletskaya Metro stations, killing 39 persons and injuring about 120.[229] The ensuing fire and smoke that filled the station created difficulties in evacuating the injured, and stopped all metro traffic for the day.[230] Police barricaded the metro, and the Emergency Situations Ministry reacted to the event.[231] President Putin and Moscow officials immediately blamed Aslan Maskhadov and Chechen rebels for the bombing, but Maskhadov denied the attack.[232]

Moscow Lubyanka / Park Kultury Metro Bombings. On the morning of March 29, 2010, female suicide bombers detonated explosives on two Moscow metro lines, killing 40 persons and injuring more than 60.[233] The first bombing took place inside a train carriage at the Lubyanka metro station, which is beneath the FSB headquarters. The bomber was positively identified as the 28 year-old wife of a Dagestani militant leader.[234] The second attack occurred inside a train carriage at the Park Kultury metro station.[235] The Park Kultury bomber was identified as the 17 year-old wife of a Dagestani militant killed by Russian forces in Dagestan in 2009.[236] Chechen rebel leader Doku Umarov claimed responsibility for the attacks to avenge killings of civilians in the North Caucasus by Russian forces, and warned of further attacks in Russia's heartland.[237]

Domodedovo International Airport Bombing. On January 24, 2011, a suicide bomber killed 35 persons and wounded more than 150 others in an attack at Moscow's

Domodedovo Airport, which is the largest of three airports serving the Russian capital.[238] No one has claimed responsibility for the attack, but as has become normal in the aftermath of similar attacks, the Kremlin leadership blamed Islamic separatists from Chechnya or the greater Caucasus area, vowing revenge for the attacks.[239]

Russian President Medvedev also blamed negligent security on the part of airport authorities for allowing the bomber to penetrate the airport, as the attack occurred at the international arrivals area of Domodedovo.[240] Medvedev gave a speech to the FSB after the attack that suggested that some FSB members might also be at fault for poor security, along with airport police and managers, and intimated that punishments should be given for those found at fault.[241] Medvedev directed more stringent checks of passengers and baggage, and stated that while this may delay passengers, that it was necessary for security.[242]

This is not the first time that Domodedovo had been used for attacks. In 2004 two female passengers boarded separate flights from Domodedovo and detonated explosives that brought down both aircraft and killed 90 persons.[243] The effects of those attacks have heightened the tension of Moscow's leadership ahead of the planned 2014 Winter Olympics in the Black Sea city of Sochi, near the North Caucasus.[244] The International Olympic Committee though, has stated they have no doubts as to Russian security forces capabilities of keeping the games safe.[245]

Growing Instability in the North Caucasus

When President Putin came to power in 1999 and invaded Chechnya to quell the rebellion, he intended to wipe out the insurgency and reduce the threat of further insurgent activity. Unfortunately, the harshness of his measures has encouraged steady attacks throughout the North Caucasus and in the Moscow region, and the insurgency

22

has continued to spread throughout the Caucasus. During Putin's tenure as President, he has instituted ever increasing anti-terrorism measures and enacted legislation that increased the powers of the police and the Russian security apparatus, including the direct appointment of governors in Russia's regions instead of democratic elections.[246] These measures have only increased opposition to Putin's methods, which have included laws that prevent news media from portraying Chechen insurgents as persons vying for independence, but instead as terrorists.[247] News media that have ignored the laws have been sanctioned or shut down.[248]

The North Caucasus region consists of seven republics, which includes Chechnya, Dagestan, Ingushetia, North Ossetia, Kabardino-Balkaria, Karachaevo-Cheressia, and Adygea.[249] In an attempt to solidify central government control of the region from the Kremlin, Russia's last President Dmitry Medvedev in January 2010 formed a new North Caucasus Federal District consisting of Chechnya, Dagestan, Ingushetia, North Ossetia, Kabardino-Balkaria, and Karachay-Cherkessia, as well as the Stavropol Krai (Krai is Russian for region).[250] Adygea continues to belong to the previously existing South Caucasus Federal District.[251]

Alexander Khloponin was appointed by Medvedev to govern the new region.[252] Khloponin is the former governor of the Krasnoyarsk region of Russia, located in western Siberia.[253] Khloponin was chosen by Medvedev to focus on economic development in the district, as he has a history of success in business, including a background in economics and finance, and also oversaw successful economic development of the Krasnoyarsk Krai.[254] Despite these credentials and potential benefit to the region and republics, Khloponin also has the power to overrule decisions of the leaders of the republics within the District.[255] This move has unsettled the local leadership and population, who see it as an attempt to lessen the authority of individual republics and centralize control of the region through Russian authority.[256]

Even as President Medvedev declared an end to counterterrorism operations in Chechnya in April 2009, violence increased in the North Caucasus between Muslims, Russian forces, and local government authorities. The death of rebel leader Shamil Basayev in 2006 in Ingushetia was hoped by Moscow's leadership to quash the spread of violence, but instead it increased, with acts of violence reportedly growing from 795 in 2008 to 1,100 in 2009, with a quadrupling of suicide bombings in 2009.[257] Suicide bombings have increased in Moscow since 2010, several of which are thought to have been carried out by the "Black Widows," women whose husbands were killed by Russian forces during the Chechen wars or disappeared during infamous Russian sweep operations.[258]

Chechnya. Violence has continued in Chechnya, but has become increasingly distant from a war of independence carried out by separatist rebels, and more an Islamic fundamentalist struggle.[259] President Putin assured this by refusing to negotiate or work with the sole moderate figure among the rebels, Aslan Maskhadov, by killing him in March 2005 in a special operation.[260] Maskhadov did reach out to the Kremlin in 1999 in an attempt to negotiate, but the attempt was abortive, as Putin's pre-condition for discussions was that Maskhadov disavow his field commander Basayev.[261]

By Putin's killing of Maskhadov, he felt he was removing the last point of resistance from Western views that the Chechens were fighting for freedom, and could from that point on characterize the fight as counterterrorism.[262] What Putin did not

24

understand was that he was simultaneously removing the last bit of moderation in the fight, and had opened the door to the entire North Caucasus fighting a war of militant fundamentalism against the federation.[263] The fight still includes a goal of independence, but independence with the freedom to practice Islam.[264]

Dagestan. Dagestan has a population of more than 2.5 million, the vast majority of whom practices Islam. Violence in Dagestan has increased since Putin announced the end of counterterrorist operations in Chechnya.[265] Violence between Dagestani security forces and militant Islamists is a common occurrence.[266] Dagestani suicide bombers, not Chechen, conducted the March 2010 attacks against the Moscow metro.[267]

Dagestan was a supply route for Chechen rebels during the first Chechen war, and was cited by the Kremlin as a reason to invade Chechnya in 1999, following Shamil Basayev's incursion into Dagestan in a failed bid to overthrow the government.[268] A significant oil pipeline, the Baku-Novorossiysk, crosses Dagestan on its way from the Caspian to the Black Seas.[269] Dagestan is an extremely mountainous area, with terrain ascending to 13,000 feet at its highest, and is heavily forested.[270] This geography is unlike what Russian forces saw during both Chechen conflicts, and limits the types of forces and weapons that Russia could employ.[271]

Dagestan's majority population is Muslim, and is a mix of Salafists and Sufis.[272] Sufism came into Dagestan during the Middle Ages, as it had throughout the Caucasus, and blended over time with local traditions.[273] The forced atheism of the Soviet period caused Sufism to go underground along with all other religions, but it reemerged after the collapse of communism in Russia.[274] It was during this period that Salafism emerged in Dagestan from Central Asia.[275]

Whereas Salafis believe that they have a direct relationship with Allah through the words of the prophet as written in the Koran, Sufis follow the instructions of their sheiks, or Imams.[276] Salafis do not agree with the Sufi tradition of supporting a secular state, and so there is tension between the nuances of the faith.[277] This has manifested itself with acts of violence against Muslims that do not practice the more strict form of Salafism, but the common enemy is the Dagestani government, which is backed by Russia.[278]

Whether Sufi or Salafi, the Dagestani Muslim population wants more autonomy from the Russian government to run their own affairs.[279] Sufis, however, are more accepting of a secular co-existence with Russian governmental authority, while Salafists want an Islamic government run according to Sharia law.[280] Russian-backed Dagestani government authorities are targeted daily by Dagestani rebels, and there are estimates of as many as 1,500 rebels in the mountains and forests of Dagestan who are being actively supported by the local population, with many thousands prepared to join them if needed.[281]

Since rebel leader Khalim Saydullayev's death in 2006, the principal rebel leader in the North Caucasus is thought to be Doku Umarov, an ethnic Chechen who is believed to be operating in Dagestan.[282] Umarov is suspected of directing several high-visibility attacks in Russia, and is actively being pursued by Russian forces.[283] Russian-backed government security forces and Russian military forces are also pursuing rebels in the Dagestani forests and having little luck in killing or capturing them.[284] If Russia cannot develop and execute an effective counterinsurgency strategy that involves more than just military force, they will be facing a spreading insurgency throughout the North Caucasus.

Ingushetia. The Republic of Ingushetia is quite small, with a mostly Muslim population of about 300,000, and has close historical ties with neighboring Chechnya.[285] Joseph Stalin deported the entire population of Ingushetia to Kazakhstan in 1944 along with the population of Chechnya, out of fear that they would collude with advancing German forces.[286] The Ingush peoples were allowed to return to their homeland in 1957 by Nikita Khrushchev.[287]

Ingushetia saw increasing insurgent violence as military and security forces in Chechnya pushed rebels out of the Chechen Republic and into the surrounding region.[288] On June 21, 2004 hundreds of Chechen and Ingushetian insurgents led by Shamil Basayev conducted a well-planned nighttime raid on the Ingushetian city of Nazran, killing more than 60 security forces and 25 civilians.[289] The insurgents attacked 15 government buildings in Nazran and surrounding towns, capturing large amounts of weapons and ammunition, and withdrawing with minimal losses.[290]

In June 2009, the President of Ingushetia, Yunus-Bek Yevkurov was severely injured when a suicide bomber attacked his vehicle.[291] In August 2009 the police headquarters in Nazran was also struck by a suicide bomber, killing 25 persons and injuring 164.[292] In November 2009 a bomb derailed a high-speed train between Moscow and St. Petersburg that killed 29 persons, and the bombing was linked to Ingushetia's chief rebel leader Alexander Tikhomirov.[293] Russian security forces in Ingushetia killed Tikhomirov in March 2010.[294]

27

The security situation generally improved in 2010 however, reportedly due to the strategy of rebel engagement being applied by Ingush President Yevkurov.[295] Yevkurov is reaching out to rebels in the republic to open channels of dialogue as opposed to the strict security measures being applied in Chechnya.[296] This strategy appears to be paying off with decreased bombings in the republic and less deaths among security forces from insurgent attack.[297] The improved security can also be attributed to the death of rebel leader Tikhomirov in 2010.[298]

North Ossetia. The North Ossetian Republic is home to approximately 709,900 people of mostly Christian background, and is the most economically developed North Caucasus republic.[299] Unfortunately, that development has not shielded the republic from insurgent violence. In August 2003 a truck bomb detonated at a military hospital in Mozdok, North Ossetia, which was serving as the Russian regional headquarters during the second Chechen war, killing 50 persons.[300]

North Ossetia's worst insurgent violence occurred in September 2004 when Ingushetian and Chechen insurgents took over 1,000 hostages at a school in Beslan, North Ossetia at the direction of Chechen rebel Shamil Basayev.[301] Basayev demanded an immediate end to the second Chechen war and the withdrawal of all Russian forces.[302] After three days Russian forces assaulted the school and during the fighting more than 330 persons died.[303] More than half of the dead were children, and hundreds more were injured.[304] The republic's most recent violence occurred in September 2010 when a car bomb struck the central market in the North Ossetian capital of Vladikavkaz, killing 17 persons and injuring over 140.[305]

Kabardino-Balkaria. The Republic of Kabardino-Balkaria is home to approximately 900,500 persons, and is a mix of Muslims and Christians.[306] The republic also fell victim to Joseph Stalin's WWII deportation ahead of German occupation, when Stalin deported the entire population of Balkars, and had their name removed from the title of the republic.[307] They were allowed to return in 1957 by Khrushchev and had their name restored.[308]

The republic has been mostly free of insurgent violence stemming from the war in Chechnya with the exception of an attack on Russian governmental buildings and security forces in the capital Nalchik in October 2005.[309] Shamil Basayev led rebels in a large-scale assault of government buildings leaving dozens dead.[310] A low-level insurgency has continued since the raid, and attacks on security forces have increased in 2010.[311]

Karachay-Cherkessia. The Republic of Karachay-Cherkessia has a population of approximately 440,000 with a mix of Muslims and Christians.[312] As with surrounding republics, it fell victim to Stalin's WWII deportation, and its citizenry were allowed to return from Kazakhstan in 1957.[313] The republic has thus far escaped effects of the regional insurgency, though Russian security forces have reportedly conducted several raids on suspected Islamic militants.[314]

Stavropol Krai. The Stavropol Krai is home to approximately 2.7 million persons of mostly Christian background.[315] The Krai (or territory in Russian) is home to a mainly Russian population, but also has a group of Muslims known as the Nogai, who are famous in Russian history for their fierce resistance to Russian rule.[316]

The Stavropol Territory has had a low-level Nogai insurgency ongoing since 2003, and the territory has had recent attacks that are disturbing considering the territories proximity to the planned 2014 Olympic Games in Sochi.[317] The games will be located less than 200 miles from Stavropol and easily accessible by insurgents.[318] The territory is heavily forested and remote, especially in the south, providing cover for insurgent activity.

In August 2005, Nogai insurgents wounded a police officer in Stavropol, and also in August two Nogai insurgents and one police officer were killed in a gunfight in the village of Yamangoi.[319] In February 2006, a two-day gun battle took place in the village of Tukui-Mektebe, located in the southeast of Stavropol near the border with Dagestan.[320] Special security police, investigating reports of insurgent activity, came under fire from the village and two police officers were killed.[321] Over the next two days Ministry of the Interior troops arrived as support, and then armored forces from Chechnya arrived with tanks and assault helicopters to clear the village.[322] After two days of fighting, seven police officers were killed and eleven wounded, while eight insurgents were killed, with several having escaped.[323]

In February 2011, two suicide bombings killed and wounded dozens of security forces in the village of Gubden, Stavropol Territory.[324] The first bomber was a female that detonated her device at the front of a local government building after being stopped by Ministry of the Interior forces.[325] The explosion killed one officer and wounded five others.[326] Several hours later, the husband of the first bomber detonated his device in a vehicle that was stopped at a police checkpoint, killing a police officer and wounding twenty-two fellow officers.[327]

Russia's reaction to this widening insurgency has been ineffective as they focus their efforts solely on police and military responses. Other methods of conflict resolution, though discussed by politicians, are almost nonexistent. The failure of the Russian government to move beyond these means, to learn from their mistakes, and to attempt to reach out to those that oppose them, has only assured further attacks. Russian security operations in Dagestan have demonstrated that Russia will use the same failed approach there as in Chechnya. This will continue to assure instability in the North Caucasus, and perhaps open a wider war for Russia, which will further harm its standing in the international community, as well as its economic fortunes at home.

Recommendations

Russia's anti-terrorism efforts have failed to get to the root causes of the proliferation of extremism and separatist movements: economic depression, massive unemployment and underemployment, years of harsh ethnicity-targeted population control measures, the use of military force as the government's principal instrument of choice, unbridled brutality, corruption, and the suppression of religious freedom. Countering these stimuli requires substantial economic assistance programs, improved security conditions and methods, better governance, and focused support from Russia and the international community.

A broad palette of sustained economic development measures must be taken. President Putin's long-term plan for this development envisages the employment of 400,000 citizens of the North Caucasus region in the oil and tourism industries by 2020.[328] This plan is an important step in the right direction, but is a drop in the bucket relative to the regions population of approximately 8.5 million.[329] It is vital however, that significant job creation be carried through to fruition in order to reduce the staggering levels of unemployment that provides fertile ground for insurgent recruitment. A concerted effort to reduce corruption at all levels is also imperative to reduce the anger and distrust of the regions population at governmental leadership, and to facilitate the economic growth that is stimulated by increased employment.

Oil Industry. Caspian oil and gas production holds the most promise for rapid employment in the region. From 1999-2005, Lukoil, a private Russian oil company, conducted exploration in the Caspian Sea and found six new oil fields with estimated deposits of 4.7 billion barrels of oil. [330] The largest field, named Vladimir Filanovsky, has been called the largest oil field found in 20 years in Russia, and contains an estimated 600 million barrels of oil and 34 billion cubic meters of gas. [331] Lukoil's president has stated that Filanovsky is expected to begin producing in 2014, and the company plans to invest 22 billion dollars in the North Caucasus within 15-16 years to develop these fields. [332]

Two pipelines currently pass through the North Caucasus, carrying crude oil from fields in the Caspian Basin to markets in Europe and abroad. The Caspian Pipeline Consortium or CPC, carries oil from the Tengiz field in Kazakhstan to the Black Sea port of Novorossiysk, which is located in Russia's Krasnodar Territory. [333] The CPC runs well north of Dagestan and Chechnya, passing through the Russian Republic of Kalymkia, as well as the Russian Territories of Stavropol and Krasnodar. [334] The CPC carries approximately 560,000 barrels per day but a planned expansion may bring the total throughput to 1.3 million barrels per day. [335]

The second pipeline transiting the North Caucasus is the Baku-Novorossiysk pipeline, running from the port city of Baku, Azerbaijan, to Novorossiysk, Krasnodar

Territory.[336] The Baku-Novorossiysk pipeline passes through Dagestan and Chechnya on its way to Novorossiysk, which has created security challenges.[337] Threats to the security of the pipeline by Chechen rebels, following the 1994-1996 war, prompted the Russian government to build a bypass around Chechnya through Dagestan.[338]

Work on the bypass began in 1999 and was completed in 2000, with a throughput of approximately 50,000 barrels a day.[339] In 2010, the Russian state-owned oil company, Rosneft, began construction of an oil refinery in the Chechen capital of Grozny, which is slated to be complete in 2014.[340] Vladimir Putin, who was Prime Minister when construction began, stated that the refinery would allow Chechnya to be a new center of the Russian oil industry.[341]

According to the U.S. Energy Information Administration (EIA), Russia contains the largest reserves of natural gas on earth, and also holds the eighth largest oil reserves.[342] In 2007, the EIA estimated that the Caspian could produce 4.3 million barrels per day on top of its already proven reserves of 17-49 billion barrels.[343]

Transporting hydrocarbons through the North Caucasus from the Caspian to the Black Sea is the most direct route for the Russian government to access markets in Europe and abroad. It is imperative for the economic vitality of Russia that the Kremlin maintains this route. Considering the amount of energy income at stake, Russia must have stability in the region to assure the flow of petroleum and to build energy infrastructure for the future.

To ensure that stability, the Kremlin leadership must provide incentives to insurgent fighters and the unemployed in the region that constitute their recruitment pool. Offering jobs to restore the existing oil and gas network, as well as long-term employment building infrastructure for future hydrocarbon flow, can be a huge enticement for insurgents to lay down their arms and return to their homes.

Winter Sports and Tourism. Other regional development opportunities abound. The high altitude of the North Caucasus Mountains lends them to the ski and winter sports industry, which is why the 2014 Winter Olympics will be held in Sochi, the capital city of Krasnodar Territory.[344] Sochi is located on the Black Sea coast, and is historically a vacation and health resort for Russia.[345]

The Russian government can take advantage of this underdeveloped region by employing local citizens to build and staff the Olympic venues and other ski and vacation resorts along the Black Sea coast and Caucasus mountain range, as well as the roads, airports, and railways leading to those resorts. The growth needed for this industry alone can open the rugged and forested region to self-sustaining commerce. The Russian government can also join with regional governments to expand the existing warm weather resorts and outdoor activities along the subtropical coast, and can work to develop winter sports along the Caucasus mountain range to make this region a true international vacation and recreation destination.

While speaking at a conference for Putin's United Russia party in July 2010, then Prime Minister Putin stated that the Russian government had invested 20 billion dollars in the North Caucasus in the past decade, and plans to create nearly a half million jobs over the next 10 years in the region.[346] Putin also plans to develop the winter sports industry along the North Caucasus mountain range by creating "ski resorts stretching from the Black to the Caspian seas.[347] To enable this, Alexander Khloponin, the governor of the North Caucasus Federal District, has developed a 15-year plan to facilitate economic development in the region.[348] The plan includes the creation of a branch of Russia's Economic Development Ministry and a state-controlled economic bank to sponsor and coordinate development projects.[349]

Sochi Olympics. Olympic security weighs heavily on the Russian government. An Olympic games free of insurgent attacks can mean a great deal of international tourism and foreign investment for the future economic viability of the region. The same is true during the construction and development of the infrastructure needed to support the games. The Russian government claims that it is providing an inordinate amount of resources towards Olympic security, but the recent shooting deaths of three persons on a ski trip to a North Caucasus resort underlines the fragility of the area. The difficulty in securing games that are situated next to a vast, undeveloped, and remote area of the North Caucasus marked by high mountains and heavy forests is problematic.[350]

Education. Pairing with universities for student and faculty educational opportunities and exchanges to explore the root causes of the insurgency, as well as religious fundamentalism and extremism, and to work assiduously to reduce those causes are also important paths to reduce the threat of future regional instability. As the conflict in the region has lasted for almost 20 years, it will take several generations of understanding and tolerance to reverse the mistrust and anger exhibited by both Russians and the peoples of the North Caucasus. The anger caused by insurgent attacks and the fear of further attack in Russia, as well as anger from North Caucasian people caused by ethnic targeting in Russia and brutal military and security operations in the North Caucasus, will not abate until security conditions improve and both sides learn, understand, and tolerate each other.

President Putin has announced plans that can potentially address these issues. In July 2010, he stated his intention to improve education opportunities in the North Caucasus by directing Russian universities to admit 1,300 North Caucasian students annually, as well as plans to build a federal university in the newly created North Caucasian Federal District.[351] Though it will take some time to put these plans into effect, they are solid steps that can have lasting positive effect on the future generations of the Russian Federation.

Security. Russia must discontinue its sole reliance on military and security operations against insurgents and insurgent leaders. Force alone has proven inadequate to the task of establishing a safe and secure environment in the region, and has, in fact, furthered regional instability by pushing Chechen insurgents out of their republic and into the surrounding region. Reaching out for dialogue with moderate rebel leaders is critical in order to understand insurgent grievances and positively address their concerns.

Local security forces need improved training to prevent the use of tactics that further inflame the population. Even so, there will be insurgents that cannot be won over. Applying a carefully managed counter-insurgency campaign with a focused special operations capability to target these individuals is a must to avoid injury to non-combatants and the unnecessary destruction of property.

Governance. Former Russian President Dmitri Medvedev made some wise appointments in 2010 that diverted from the common practice of placing local strongmen like Chechnya's Ramzan Kadyrov or Russian military and security leaders into positions of power in the region. By appointing Alexander Khloponin, who has a background in economics and finance as governor of the North Caucasus Federal District, Medvedev signaled to the region his intent to shift away from purely military and security means of regional pacification to economic development.[352] This development can address one of the major underlying causes of the insurgency, which is widespread unemployment. By developing the region economically, Khloponin can get those unemployed back to work and provide them financial security and a reason to lay down their arms.[353]

Medvedev also appointed Yunus-bek Yevkurov as the President of Ingushetia.[354] Though Yevkurov has a military background as a paratrooper, he has proven to be an effective administrator and a tolerant and understanding leader who has continually reached out to insurgents and their families to induce them to give up the fight.[355] Remarkably, even after an assassination attempt by insurgents that nearly killed him, Yevkurov forgave his attackers and engaged them to understand their grievances so he could address them.[356]

The Russian government can improve upon this successful template by choosing local leaders as deputies of Russian appointees. The deputies would have a deep understanding of the regions history, language, culture, religion, and ethnic groups and clans, and can share this knowledge with the appointees. This divestiture of power down from the central Russian authority can also demonstrate to the local population that they have a voice.

Russian leadership also needs to be more amenable to the practice of moderate Islam and to state publicly that they understand that Islam and those who practice it are not the problem, but the insurgency is. Further, local Russian appointees as well as the

Kremlin leadership must engage directly with Muslim religious leaders and show their support, which will help mitigate the insurgent message that Russian operations target Muslims, as opposed to simply targeting rebel violence.

International Support. Russia must also engage the international community for help in rebuilding Chechnya, and to restore stability in the North Caucasus. Direct foreign investment in the oil and tourism industries can provide local jobs. A shorter oil pipeline running between the Caspian and Black Seas in a stable North Caucasus can be an attractive alternative to the more costly maintenance and security requirements needed for a longer pipeline around the region. Getting in on the ground floor of a nascent ski and tourism industry can also be an attractive opportunity for foreign investors, but the security situation must first be stable before foreign investors are likely to risk their money.

Finally, allowing relief agencies and non-governmental organizations (NGOs) into the region can also be a stabilizing factor, by providing the basics needed to those displaced and impoverished by violence, especially in Chechnya. Permitting organizations such as the United States Agency for International Development (USAID) into the region can provide desperately needed humanitarian assistance to those suffering, but can also facilitate American investment in the region ahead of the Sochi Winter Olympics in 2014. More than anything else, providing job prospects to the estimated 50-75% of the population that is unemployed[357] will provide regional stability by offering an alternative joining the ranks of the insurgency.

Risk to Russia of a Prosperous North Caucasus

What are the risks to Russia of an economically prosperous North Caucasus? A prosperous and united North Caucasus region could one day seek independence from

Russia and deny, or at least limit, Russia's access to the region. Is this a realistic prospect? Quite possibly, but the damage would be minimal. Even if Russia were to cede independence to a unified North Caucasus in the future, Russia would still have access to the Black and Caspian Seas through the Rostov Oblast (Region), and Kalmykia, respectively.[358]

This geographical footprint provides Russia with access to the Black Sea for its naval presence, as well as Black Sea resort areas and oil and natural gas infrastructure. It also provides access to the Caspian fishing industry and Russia's oil and gas infrastructure in the Caspian Sea via the Kalmykia coast.[359] Unfortunately, losing the region would mean losing the Baku-Novorossiysk oil pipeline, which runs from the Caspian port city of Baku, Azerbaijan, to Novorossiysk, which is located on the Black Sea coast of the Krasnodar Territory.[360]

The Baku-Novorossiysk pipeline passes through Dagestan and Chechnya on its way to Novorossiysk.[361] A new pipeline, though costly, would have to be built above the North Caucasus to replace the Baku-Novorossiysk pipeline. However, Lukoil's current exploration of Caspian Basin oil is focused entirely offshore, and future oil could therefore be diverted through a new pipeline from the offshore oil fields through Kalmykia, then above the region through Rostov and on to the Black Sea port of Novorossiysk.[362]

An independent North Caucasus could also diminish Russian influence in the region, if the North Caucasian government chose to do business with regional and international partners to the exclusion of Russia, or in competition with Russia. For now, Russia enjoys a monopoly of influence in the region through the direct appointment of the Head of the North Caucasus Federal District, as well as the appointment of governors to the republics.[363] Losing the region would mean losing this exclusive authority and access.

Russia could also stand to lose its current infrastructure, as well as the infrastructure that is being built as part of President Putin's economic recovery plan for the region.[364] Over the next 10 years, President Putin is planning on building a university, oil infrastructure, and a vast array of ski resorts cutting through the region along the tops of the Caucasus mountain range.[365]Since these ongoing and future projects are being built with a mix of funds from the Russian state budget as well as Foreign Direct Investment, it is uncertain how ownership would be resolved if the North Caucasus became independent.[366]

Despite these risks, there is great benefit to having an economically developed North Caucasus, regardless of the status of its independence. A prosperous North Caucasus should bring stability to the region, and a thriving economy will provide jobs. Reducing the high level of unemployment among North Caucasian youth[367] should undercut the ability of militants to recruit them, and this could lead to a decrease in violence within, and outside of the region. This is a goal worthy of Russia's best efforts at economically developing the North Caucasus.

Conclusion

The Russian government has failed in its attempts to prevent further attacks by rebels from Chechnya and the North Caucasus against its interests, and to stop a widening insurgency in the North Caucasus. Bombings and attacks continue despite the Kremlin's direct role in facing these threats. This continuing conflict is a direct result of the Russian government's heavy-handed tactics throughout the federation, and its failure to see the long-term negative impact of those tactics.

While measures such as ethnic profiling and aggressive military tactics mollify the majority Russian population in the short-term, they only serve to further exacerbate the problems that face the Russian government. President Putin paid lip service to the fundamental causes of these threats, as did Russia's previous President, Dmitry Medvedev. Both men publicly maintained that Russia and the international community must be united in targeting the roots of terrorism and extremism, such as poverty and hopelessness shared by many in the world, while continuing to focus their efforts solely on military solutions and population control measures.[368]

Attacks from the North Caucasus will continue to be directed against Russia. Russia must learn from its mistakes and broaden its responses to more than military ones. The reality of continued attacks means that a carefully managed counter-insurgency campaign must be maintained. A focused special operations capability must also be designed to remove those who cannot be won over, and whose aims are to motivate and recruit new members and continue targeting Russia.

Russia must also engage in a sustained public relations effort to "win the hearts and minds" of the Federation, both in Russia and the North Caucasus. Russia must also continue to try and work with the political leadership of Chechnya, Dagestan, and the North Caucasus region, even if they are insurgent leaders, and forgo unilateral combat operations as the primary instrument of choice. Opening a dialogue with regional leaders, including rebel leaders where possible is important in order to understand how to effectively rebuild as well as govern the region.

Both the insurgents and local leadership want more autonomy. Granting more autonomy by appointing local leaders into positions of authority can be an effective self-policing measure for the Russian government, reducing local hatred and risk of attack directed against appointed Russian leaders, provided that Russian central authority (the newly created North Caucasus Federal District and the Kremlin)[369] maintains overall district control, and that control is recognized by local leaders.

Russia's continued use of the military instrument of power as the sole tool for conflict resolution in the North Caucasus is a recipe for disaster. The military alone cannot solve the diverse and complex problems that contribute to extremism and insurgency. Severe population control measures against Caucasians throughout the Federation must cease. Iron-fisted and direct rule from the central authority in the Kremlin is not working. Power needs to be divested to local leadership in combination with a well-crafted plan to check corruption, end atrocities, gain and maintain security through improved training and supervision of locally-recruited military and police forces, provide a package of economic aid, and stimulate job growth. Until then the North Caucasus remains a fertile ground for widening Islamic extremism and provides a direct threat to Russia's future stability and security.

Endnotes

[1] Gregory Freeze, eds., *Russia: A History*, (Oxford, NY: Oxford University Press, 1997) 405.

[2] Ibid., 413.

[3] Joseph Stalin died In March 1953, after serving 31 years as the General Secretary of the Communist Party in the Union of Soviet Socialist Republics (USSR) – Ibid., 349. The Stalinist period was marked with the tyranny of purges and labor camps, the consolidation of power around Stalin himself by weakening the existing centers of government, the primacy of

industrialization over agriculture, which left little food for the people, and a massive military budget that created a substantial state deficit – Ibid., 348-349.

Nikita Khrushchev assumed power as the First Secretary of the Soviet Central Committee of the Communist Party of the Soviet Union (CPSU) after Stalin's death, and immediately instituted sweeping changes to virtually all aspects of Soviet life – Ibid., 349. Khrushchev diverted money from the heavy industry budget and pushed it to the agricultural sector, resulting in substantially increased harvests – Ibid., 351-352. Khrushchev also reduced the number of central government employees, and decentralized power to the republics. This move improved the ability of republics to control their output, resulting in a considerable increase of industrial productivity – Ibid., 352-353.

Khrushchev also initiated a campaign of de-Stalinization, exposing the repressive and secretive police state that Stalin cultivated, including details of the victims of Stalin's oppression within the Soviet government and society, as well as the republics – Ibid., 356. De-Stalinization incited anger inside the Soviet Union as well as the republics, and the realization of Stalin's staggering atrocities against his own people led directly to the revolt in Hungary and its brutal suppression by Soviet military forces in 1956 – Ibid., 357.

Khrushchev was unceremoniously removed from his position and replaced by Leonid Brezhnev in 1964, after a series of reversals stemming from his programs of decentralization and democratization. Among the issues were the foreign policy debacles of the 1961 Berlin wall and Cuban missile crises – Ibid., 363-364, the massive amount of defense spending to the detriment of the economy and a rapid decline in agricultural output, and resistance to his decentralization of power to the republics by the Soviet ruling elite – Ibid., 363-368.

The Brezhnev era was marked largely by rapid reversals of Khrushchev's policy, consolidation of power by Brezhnev, and a sharp economic decline in the USSR - 368-377. The Brezhnev era saw the brutal repression of Czech nationalists during the 1968 "Prague Spring," as well as Détente, which enlarged trade with the western world, and lessened the tension between the Soviet Union and the United States – Ibid., 370; 377-378. Détente ended in 1979 when the Soviet Union invaded Afghanistan – Ibid.

Brezhnev died in 1982 and was replaced in rapid succession by Yuri Andropov, and then Konstantin Chernenko, both of whom died within three years time – Ibid., 381-382. In 1985 Mikhail Gorbachev assumed the position as General Secretary of the CPSU – Ibid., 382. Gorbachev was the principal architect for the Soviet policies of Perestroika (restructuring), Glasnost (openness), and Democratizatsiia (democratization) – 384. By introducing these three policies in an attempt to reform the stagnated Soviet system, Gorbachev was unknowingly setting in motion feelings of nationalism and independence that would see the collapse of the Berlin Wall and the end of the Soviet Union.

Gorbachev had no intention of causing the disintegration of the USSR. His vision was to breathe new life into communism in the Soviet Union by reverting to its ideals under Lenin – Ibid. His belief was that by reforming and rebuilding the institutions of government (Perestroika), being open and transparent in governance (Glasnost), and having participatory rule, guided by a strong center (Democratizatsiia), that communism in the USSR could be revitalized – Ibid.

Gorbachev's plans for a wide-reaching transformation of the entire Soviet system quickly ran into trouble from the party elite. Gorbachev believed that the stagnation of the system stemmed from an entrenched bureaucracy of the Soviet central planning and governance system that benefited the few, and fostered corruption, waste, and a host of other excesses - 384-390. This perceived attack on the central Soviet elite triggered their suspicion and resistance to change, and caused a fracture between themselves and the more radical reformers, among who were Gorbachev as well as Boris Yeltsin, who had been appointed first party secretary of Moscow in December 1985 – Ibid., 384-392.

In June 1988 Gorbachev presided over a central party conference that further devolved power to local organizations, instituted contested elections at all party levels, and established the position of President within the central party – Ibid., 392. The party membership then appointed Gorbachev as the first President – Ibid.. Gorbachev however, was still not satisfied with the pace of reforms, and was frustrated by the communist central party's authority to resist change.

In order to overcome this resistance Gorbachev needed to officially separate the roles of the central party and the state. In November 1988 the USSR Supreme Soviet, which at the time was the highest legislative body in the USSR whose members were appointed by the central party, established a new organization called the Congress of People's Deputies (CPD) – 393. The CPD was a freely elected organization comprising two bodies; the CPD and a smaller Supreme Soviet, to be elected by the CPD. The CPD was to act as the congress of the Soviet Union, meeting twice a year to consider significant issues of the USSR, with the smaller Supreme Soviet acting as the permanent legislative branch of the state – Ibid.

The USSR CPD held its first elections in March 1989, during which Boris Yeltsin won the post of Moscow Deputy, and was then further elected to the Supreme Soviet – 394. The CPD elected Mikhail Gorbachev as the President of the USSR after it convened – Ibid. The establishment of a freely elected CPD both marginalized and angered the CPSU, though central party members still comprised a large portion of the deputies of the CDP and the Supreme Soviet – Ibid., 393-401.

As a result of internal tensions within the CPSU resulting from the formation of the USSR CPD, the communist party began to fractionalize between party hard-liners resisting reform, Gorbachev who pressed retention of, but reformation of the party, and Boris Yeltsin, who advocated for state independence and democracy. At the 28th Congress of the CPSU in July 1990, Gorbachev was re-elected as party General Secretary, but Yeltsin resigned from the party, leading his democratically minded followers to form the Russian Congress of People's Deputies (Russian CPD).

A series of setbacks struck the USSR beginning in 1989. Soviet troops withdrew from Afghanistan in February 1989 after ten years of war and high casualties – Ibid., 404. The Berlin Wall separating East and West Germany was opened in October 1989, following a statement by Gorbachev during a trip to East Germany that Soviet forces would not be used in defense of communist regimes – Ibid., 405. Serious fissures formed in the economy of the USSR as a result of the weight of defense spending and attempted structural changes under Perestroika, including shortages of goods, forced rationing, and the inflation of the Ruble – Ibid., 401-404. In the spring of 1990 Latvia, Lithuania, and Estonia, declared their independence from the USSR – 408.

In May 1990, Boris Yeltsin's Russian CPD met and declared the independence of Russia as a sovereign republic – 407. The Russian CPD also proposed the post of President of the

Russian Federation, and with the support of Gorbachev as General Secretary of the USSR, Russia elected Boris Yeltsin as President of the Russian Federation in March 1991 – Ibid.. On March 17, 1991 Ukrainian voters passed a referendum declaring their independence from the USSR, and on March 31, 1991 Georgia followed suit with a vote to declare its independence – 407-410.

On August 18, 1991 eight members of the CPSU who were against Gorbachev's reforms initiated a coup against Gorbachev while he was vacationing in the Crimea – 411. The coup plotters, including Gorbachev's Vice President Gennady Yanayev, as well as the head of the KGB, Ministry of Defense, Ministry of Interior, and other members of government, demanded that Gorbachev resign, but he refused – Ibid. The coup members placed Gorbachev under house arrest, and on August 19 sent military forces into downtown Moscow to occupy the Russian White House and arrest Boris Yeltsin – Ibid.

Yeltsin was able to avoid arrest and went to the White House, addressing the Russian people from a tank, asking for their support and demanding the release of Gorbachev and the capitulation of the coup plotters – Ibid. After the military refused to fire on the civilians and supported Yeltsin, the coup collapsed and on August 21 Gorbachev was released from house arrest and returned to Moscow – Ibid.

Yeltsin's bold action during the coup sealed his popularity and further diminished the power of the CPSU and Mikhail Gorbachev. In early December 1991, Boris Yeltsin and the leaders of Ukraine and Belarus formed the Commonwealth of Independent States (CIS), and on December 21 the CIS was officially established – Ibid., 413. On December 25, 1991 Gorbachev resigned, and on December 31, 1991 the USSR was formally dissolved – Ibid.

Capitalizing on the failed coup and the unrest in the Ukraine and Belarus, Chechnya declared its independence from the USSR in November 1991 – Ibid., 443. Unlike those peripheral republics, however, Chechnya was an integral part of Russia, and Chechen independence threatened Russia's territorial integrity – Ibid., 9. The new Russian government declared Chechnya's independence unconstitutional, but was able to do little else while it focused on its economic woes from 1991-1993 - Anna Politkovskaya, *A Small Corner Of Hell, Dispatches From Chechnya* (Chicago and London: The University of Chicago Press), 18.

By 1994, public order had eroded – Ibid, and was threatening Chechnya's substantial ethnic Russian population - "The Conflict in Chechnya," House of Commons Library, Research Paper 00/14, 7 February 2000, http://www.parliament.uk/briefing-papers/RP00-14.pdf, 9 (accessed January 22, 2012). Also threatened was the important oil industry in Chechnya that included refineries in the capital city of Grozny, and pipelines running through the republic from the Caspian to the Black Seas - Freeze, *Russia: A History*, 419; Mairbek Vatchagaev, "Oil in Chechnya: A Brief History," The Jamestown Foundation, North Caucasus Analysis Volume 9 Issue 15, April 17, 2008, http://www.jamestown.org/single/?no_cache=1&tx_ttnews%5Btt_news%5D=4870, (accessed April 8, 2012). Chechen secession also posed the risk of starting a domino effect among other republics seeking their own independence - Anna Politkovskaya, *A Small Corner Of Hell, Dispatches From Chechnya,* 17-19.

Yeltsin therefore sent Russian military forces into Chechnya in a vicious two-year military operation lasting from 1994-1996 - Olga Oliker, *Russia's Chechen Wars 1994-2000, Lessons from Urban Combat*, (Arroyo Center: Rand), 1-2, in order to preserve the integrity of the Russian

Federation - Sebastian Smith, *Allah's Mountains, The Battle For Chechnya*, (New York, Tauris Parke Paperbacks), xxvi-xxvii. Hostilities between Russian forces and Chechen rebels were repeated by President Putin in a 1999-2009 war that lay waste to the Chechen capital city of Grozny - Constance A. Philpot, "The North Caucasus: Russian Roulette on Europe's Borders," *Parameters* (Summer 2010): 87-88, caused the displacement of approximately 200,000 refugees – Ibid., 94, and killed an estimated 100,000 people, among both combatants and non-combatants – Ibid.

[4] Freeze, *Russia: A History*, 419; Mairbek Vatchagaev, "Oil in Chechnya: A Brief History," The Jamestown Foundation, North Caucasus Analysis Volume 9 Issue 15, April 17, 2008, http://www.jamestown.org/single/?no_cache=1&tx_ttnews%5Btt_news%5D=4870 (accessed April 8, 2012).

[5] Ibid., 9.

[6] Politkovskaya, *A Small Corner Of Hell, Dispatches From Chechnya*, 18.

[7] Ibid.

[8] "The Conflict in Chechnya," 9.

[9] Freeze, *Russia: A History*, 443.

[10] Politkovskaya, *A Small Corner Of Hell, Dispatches From Chechnya*, 17-19.

[11] Oliker, *Russia's Chechen Wars 1994-2000, Lessons from Urban Combat*, 1-2.

[12] Smith, *Allah's Mountains, The Battle For Chechnya*, xxvi-xxvii.

[13] Constance A. Philpot, "The North Caucasus: Russian Roulette on Europe's Borders," *Parameters Online* (Summer 2010): 87-88, http://www.carlisle.army.mil/usawc/Parameters/Articles/2010summer/Philpot.pdf (accessed March 12, 2012).

[14] "Russia threatens to retake Chechnya," BBC News, World, Europe, November 3, 1999, http://news.bbc.co.uk/2/hi/europe/503636.stm (accessed March 18, 2012).

[15] Svante E. Cornell, "Russia's Gridlock in Chechnya: "Normalization" or Deterioration?" Center for OSCE Research, Yearbook 2004, http://www.core-hamburg.de/documents/yearbook/english/04/Cornell.pdf, 255-258 (accessed March 12, 2012).

[16] Philpot, "The North Caucasus: Russian Roulette on Europe's Borders," 92.

[17] "Russia: Investigate Sexual Violence by Troops in Chechnya," Human Rights Watch, April 10, 2002, http://www.hrw.org/news/2002/04/09/russia-investigate-sexual-violence-troops-chechnya, (accessed March 31, 2012); Russia: Making Justice Count in Chechnya, Implementation of European Court of Human Rights Rulings against Russia, Human Rights Watch, November 14, 2011, http://www.hrw.org/news/2011/11/14/russia-making-justice-count-chechnya (accessed March 31, 2012).

[18] "UN condemns Russia over Chechnya," BBC News, World, Europe, April 20, 2001, http://news.bbc.co.uk/2/hi/europe/1288414.stm (accessed March 31, 2012); UN Commission Urged to Act on Chechnya, Human Rights Watch, March 14, 2002, http://www.hrw.org/news/2002/03/13/un-commission-urged-act-chechnya (accessed March 31, 2012).

[19] "North Caucasus: Guide to a volatile region," BBC News, Europe, January 25, 2011, http://www.bbc.co.uk/news/world-europe-12274023 (accessed February 9, 2012).

[20] Rajan Menon, "Russia's hot spot," Los Angeles Times, March 31, 2010, http://articles.latimes.com/2010/mar/31/opinion/la-oe-menon31-2010mar31 (accessed March 12, 2012).

[21]

Chechnya and N. Caucasus	Event	Russia
Accused of Nazi Collaboration	WWII	Stalin Deports Chechens
Hope for independence	Fall of the Berlin Wall	Democratic reformers vs. communist hard-liners
Chechnya declares independence NOV 91	AUG 91 anti-reform coup	Gorbachev held in Crimea under house arrest; Yeltsin goes to White House, causes coup collapse
Harsh methods demoralize Chechen population and destroys infrastructure	Yelstin sends troops to Chechnya from 1994-96; Dudayev killed by missile	Mostly conscript soldiers are decimated by Chechens; Russian population horrified by troop losses
Chechens separatists are labeled "terrorists" by Russia	New Russian Anti-terrorism Law	Law gives government wide authorities and latitude
Kidnapping rampant; widespread lawlessness; Basayev and Khattab form parallel government	Moderate rebel leader Aslan Maskhadov elected as Chechen President	Yeltsin congratulates Maskhadov
Maskhadov denies Chechen involvement; no evidence of Chechen involvement. Chechens targeted in Russia	Apartment bombings SEP 99; Operation Whirlwind in Moscow; Dagestani incursions by Shamil Basayev	Putin accuses Chechen rebels of bombings; Putin uses bombings as pretext for second war; repression of Caucasians in Moscow
Basayev and Khattab link up with Dagestani militants; Maskhadov denounces Basayev	2ND Chechen War	Moscow demands "terrorists" extradited; Russian forces raze Grozny and occupy city; Akhmad Kadyrov appointed interim leader by Putin

Rebels deny involvement	Pushkinskaya Metro bombing	Zhirinovsky supporters display banner in Moscow stating "A good Chechen is a dead Chechen"
Chechen rebels take over 800 hostages in Moscow Dubrovka Theater; demand end to war; Russian troop withdrawal; negotiations with Maskhadov; backlash against Chechens and other Caucasians	Moscow Dubrovka theater Hostage Crisis OCT 02	Russian Special Forces assault theater, kill rebels; 129 hostages die from unknown gas infiltrated into building before assault; accusations about gas use and lack of medical support during crisis
No responsibility claimed	Three additional Metro bombings	Chechen rebels blamed
Did not claim responsibility	Moscow Domodedevo Airport bombing; 35 dead, 180 injured	Medyedev blames Chechens; suggests lax airport security allowed suicide bomber to strike

[22] Smith, *Allah's Mountains, The Battle For Chechnya*, xxvi-xxvii.

[23] Philpot, "The North Caucasus: Russian Roulette on Europe's Borders," 87, 97; Mairbek Vatchagaev, "Oil in Chechnya: A Brief History," Volume 9 Issue 15.

[24] Anna Pechlivanidou, "Russian crude oil pipelines and their impact on tankers demand," Erasmus University Rotterdam, http://www.maritimeeconomics.com/system/files/downloads/ Thesis_PechA.pdf (accessed April 8, 2012), 17.

[25] Philpot, "The North Caucasus: Russian Roulette on Europe's Borders," 87.

[26] Clifford J. Levy, "Russia Faces 3-Year Race to Secure Site of Olympics," The New York Times, March 7, 2011, http://www.nytimes.com/2011/03/08/world/europe/08sochi.html?_r=1 (accessed March 12, 2012).

[27] Ibid.

[28] Ibid.

[29] Valery Dzutsev, "Leader of the Caucasus Emirate Vows to Stop Attacks Against Russian Civilians," *Eurasia Daily Monitor Online*, Volume 9 Issue 24 (February 3, 2012), http://www.jamestown.org/programs/nca/single/?tx_ttnews%5Btt_news%5D=38970&tx_ttnews %5BbackPid%5D=24&cHash=77572f0fd05e51237e58c4c05ab56240 (accessed March 12, 2012).

[30] Smith, *Allah's Mountains, The Battle For Chechnya*, xxvi-xxvii.

[31] Philpot, "The North Caucasus: Russian Roulette on Europe's Borders," 94.

[32] Ibid.

[33] "Chechen conflict could spread to neighboring republics: Russia," AFP, Johnson's Russia List #1, http://www.cdi.org/russia/johnson/4298.html##1 (accessed January 22, 2012).

[34] Nikolaos Dendias, "The situation of IDPs and returnees in the North Caucasus region," Council of Europe Parliamentary Assembly, March 5, 2012, http://assembly.coe.int/ASP/Doc/ XrefViewHTML.asp?FileID=12950&Language=EN (accessed April 14, 2012).

[35] Gregory Feifer, "Radicalization Splitting Society In Russia's North Caucasus," Radio Free Europe Radio Liberty, November 4, 2012, http://www.rferl.org/articleprintview/24381757.html (accessed April 13, 2012).

[36] Cornell, "Russia's Gridlock in Chechnya: "Normalization" or Deterioration?" 255.

[37] "North Caucasus: Guide to a volatile region."

[38] Ibid; Menon, "Russia's hot spot."

[39] "OGPSS - Oil production from the North Caucasus."; Shirin Akiner, "Politics of Energy in the Caspian Sea Region," Europa World Online, http://www.europaworld.com/entry/eer.essay.2, 12 (accessed November 3, 2011).

[40] Heather Field, "The Geopolitics of Caspian Oil," *The Contemporary Europe Research Centre Online*, University of Melbourne, Russian and Euro-Asian Bulletin, Vol.9, No.2, (March-April 2000), http://cerc.unimelb.edu.au/bulletin/00mar.htm (accessed March 18, 2012).

[41] David Hearst, "Moscow and Grozny edge closer to war: Russian tanks roll to border as bombed Chechens threaten to retaliate," The Guardian, September 24, 1999, http://www.guardian.co.uk/world/1999/sep/25/russia.chechnya?INTCMP=ILCNETTXT3487 (accessed April 20, 2012).

[42] Ioannis Vichos and Sotirios Karampampas, "The security situation in North Caucasus and the energy factor."

[43] Ibid.

[44] "The Conflict in Chechnya," 9-13.

[45] Smith, *Allah's Mountains, The Battle For Chechnya*, xxvi-xxvii; Ibid., xxvi; xxix-xxxi; "The Conflict in Chechnya," 11.

[46] Ibid., 15-20.

[47] Smith, *Allah's Mountains, The Battle For Chechnya*, xxvi-xxvii.

[48] Philpot, "The North Caucasus: Russian Roulette on Europe's Borders," 87-90, 92-94.

[49] "Chechnya," Encyclopedia Britannica Online, January 28, 2012, http://www.britannica.com/EBchecked/topic/108244/Chechnya (accessed February 5, 2012).

[50] Ibid.

[51] "Regions and territories: Chechnya."

[52] "Chechnya."

[53] Ibid.

[54] Ibid; "Timeline: Chechnya," BBC News, January 19, 2011, http://news.bbc.co.uk/go/pr/fr/-/2/hi/asia-pacific/country_profiles/2357267.stm (accessed February 5, 2012).

[55] "The Conflict in Chechnya," 13.

[56] Ibid., 12.

[57] Ibid.

[58] Ibid., 12-13.

[59] Ibid; "Timeline: Chechnya."

[60] "Duma," Encyclopedia Britannica, http://www.britannica.com/EBchecked/topic/173419/Duma (accessed April 15, 2012).

[61] Petrishchev, "Russian Legislation and the Fight Against Terrorism."

[62] Ibid.

[63] Ibid.

[64] Ibid.

[65] Ibid.

[66] Malik, "Tatarstan's Treaty with Russia: Autonomy or Independence."

[67] Freeze, *Russia: A History*, 407-410.

[68] Malik, "Tatarstan's Treaty with Russia: Autonomy or Independence."

[69] Petrishchev, "Russian Legislation and the Fight Against Terrorism."

[70] "On the Fight Against Terrorism," Russian Federation Federal Law No. 130-FZ signed by Russian Federation President Boris Yeltsin, 25 July 1998, Russian Intelligence-Related Legal Documents, http://www.fas.org/irp/world/russia/docs/law_980725.htm (accessed January 8, 2012).

[71] Ibid.

[72] Ibid.

[73] Colonel Sergey A. Kulikov, "The Tactics of Insurgent Groups in the Republic of Chechnya," Foreign Military Studies Office, Fort Leavenworth, Kansas, December 2002, http://fmso.leavenworth.army.mil/documents/chechinsurgtact.htm (accessed April 2, 2012).

[74] Lev Levinson, Human Rights Institute, "Governance as a Counter-Terrorist Operation: Notes on the Russian legislation against terrorism," January 2007, http://ejp.icj.org/IMG/Levinson.pdf (accessed January 8, 2012).

[75] Ibid.

[76] Committee to Protect Journalists, "Authorities issue warning to newspaper over Chechnya interview," February 9, 2005, http://www.ifex.org/russia/2005/02/10/authorities_issue_warning_to_newspaper (accessed January 8, 2012).

[77] Ibid.

[78] "Timeline: Chechnya."

[79] Fiona Graham, "Key figures," The Telegraph, October 28, 2002, http://www.telegraph.co.uk/news/1399554/Key-figures.html, (accessed April 10, 2012); "Aslan Maskhadov, Former Chechen President," Background People, Russia Profile.org, June 24, 2012, http://russiaprofile.org/bg_people/resources_whoiswho_alphabet_m_maskhadov.html (accessed April 19, 2012).

[80] S. Frederick Starr, "A Solution For Chechnya," The Washington Post with Foreign Policy, World, September 17, 2004, http://www.washingtonpost.com/wp-dyn/articles/A27550-2004Sep16.html, (accessed April 10, 2012); Charles Gurin, "Islamist Named Formal Head of Chechen Resistance," The Jamestown Foundation, March 10, 2005, http://www.jamestown.org/single/?no_cache=1&tx_ttnews%5Btt_news%5D=27674 (accessed April 10, 2012).

[81] "The Conflict in Chechnya," 13.

[82] "Timeline: Chechnya."

[83] Ibid.

[84] Ibid; Anna Matveeva, "Chechnya: Drive for Independence or Hotbed for Islamic Terrorism?" Searching for Peace in Europe and Eurasia, 2002, http://conflict-prevention.net/page.php?id=40&formid=73&action=show&surveyid=52 (accessed April 10, 2012).

[85] "Amelia Gentleman, "Russia's shockwave of terror," The Guardian, September 14, 1999, http://www.guardian.co.uk/world/1999/sep/14/russia.ameliagentleman?INTCMP=SRCH (accessed January 21, 2012).

[86] Gregory Feifer, "Ten Years On, Troubling Questions Linger Over Russian Apartment Bombings," Radio Free Europe Radio Liberty, January 15, 2012, http://www.rferl.org/content/Ten_Years_On_Troubling_Questions_Linger_Over_Russian_Apartment_Bombings/1818652.html (accessed 14 January 2012).

[87] Amelia Gentleman, "Chechen bomb suspects take the dock," July 12, 2001, The Guardian, http://www.guardian.co.uk/world/2001/jul/12/worlddispatch.ameliagentleman (accessed January 13, 2012).

[88] Ibid; "Chechnya," Encyclopedia Britannica Online, January 28, 2012, http://www.britannica.com/EBchecked/topic/108244/Chechnya (accessed January 22, 2012).

[89] "Security clampdown in Russia ," BBC News, World, Europe, September 15, 1999, http://news.bbc.co.uk/2/hi/europe/448005.stm (accessed April 10, 2012).

[90] David Satter, "The Shadow of Ryazan," Hudson Institute, May 1, 2002, http://www.hudson.org/index.cfm?fuseaction=publication_details&id=2089 (accessed March 18, 2012).

[91] Smith, *Allah's Mountains, The Battle For Chechnya*, xxvi-xxvii.

[92] Jamie Dettmer, "Did Putin's Agents Plant the Bombs?" CBS Interactive Business Network Resource Library, April 17, 2000, http://findarticles.com/p/articles/mi_m1571/is_14_16/ai_61892243/pg_2/?tag=content;col1 (accessed April 11, 2012).

[93] Julius Strauss, "Secret at the heart of Putin's rise to power," The Telegraph, March 13, 2004, http://www.telegraph.co.uk/news/worldnews/europe/russia/1456763/Secret-at-the-heart-of-Putins-rise-to-power.html (accessed April 11, 2012).

[94] Peter Heinlen, "Russia Election/Bombings," Voice of America, March 22, 2000, http://www.fas.org/irp/news/2000/03/000322-fsb1.htm (accessed January 13, 2012), 2.

[95] Satter, "The Shadow of Ryazan."

[96] Ibid.

[97] Heinlen, "Russia Election/Bombings."

[98] Ibid.

[99] Ibid.

[100] Ibid.

[101] Ibid.

[102] "Russian tycoon blames Moscow for blasts," BBC News, World Europe, March 6, 2002, http://news.bbc.co.uk/2/hi/europe/1857060.stm (accessed January 13, 2012).

[103] Ibid.

[104] Ibid.

[105] "FSB Chief Accuses Berezovsky of financing Chechen Rebels," The Jamestown Monitor, Volume: 8 Issue 18, January 25, 2002, http://www.jamestown.org/single/

?no_cache=1&tx_ttnews%5Btt_news%5D=23867&tx_ttnews%5BbackPid%5D=216 (accessed 14 January 2012).

[106] Christopher Kenneth, "FSB threatens Berezovsky with international arrest warrant," The Russia Journal, Issue 146, January 2, 2002, http://www.russiajournal.com/node/5807 (accessed January 14, 2012.

[107] Strauss, "Secret at the heart of Putin's rise to power."

[108] Ibid; "Ex-KGB officer poisoning probed," BBC News, November 19, 2006, http://news.bbc.co.uk/2/hi/uk_news/6162562.stm, (accessed April 11, 2012); Gregory Feifer, "Russia: Three Years Later, Moscow Apartment Bombings Remain Unsolved," Radio Free Europe Radio Liberty, September 6, 2002, http://www.rferl.org/content/article/1100714.html (accessed April 11, 2012).

[109] Gentleman, "Chechen bomb suspects take the dock."

[110] Feifer, "Ten Years On, Troubling Questions Linger Over Russian Apartment Bombings."

[111] Gentleman, "Chechen bomb suspects take the dock."

[112] Ibid.

[113] Ibid.

[114] Ibid.

[115] Peter Graff, "2 Men Given Life for Buinaksk Bombings," March 20, 2001, The St. Petersburg Times, http://www.sptimes.ru/archive/pdf/654.pdf (accessed January 14, 2012).

[116] Ibid.

[117] Gentleman, "Chechen bomb suspects take the dock."

[118] Ibid.

[119] "Russia, Country Reports on Human Rights Practices," U.S. Department of State, March 4, 2002, http://www.state.gov/j/drl/rls/hrrpt/2001/eur/8331.htm (accessed April 11, 2012).

[120] Mark Tran, "45 die in Moscow 'terrorist' explosion," Guardian.co.uk, September 13, 1999, http://www.guardian.co.uk/world/1999/sep/13/russia.marktran, (accessed January 21, 2012); "Security clampdown in Russia," BBC News, World, Europe, September 15, 1999, http://news.bbc.co.uk/2/hi/europe/448005.stm (accessed January 21, 2012).

[121] Ibid.

[122] "Suspected bomb in Truck Russian apartment building blast," CNN.com, September 16, 1999, http://translate.google.com/translate?hl=en&sl=es&tl=en&u=http%3A%2F%2F www.danielestulin.com%2Fwp-content%2Fuploads%2F1999.pdf (accessed January 21, 2012).

[123] Ibid.

[124] Fred Weir, "Fred Weir on treatment of Chechens," Johnson's Russia List #3555, October 10, 1999, http://www.cdi.org/russia/johnson/3555.html#1 (accessed January 21, 2012).

[125] Ibid.

[126] Ibid.

[127] Ibid.

[128] Ibid.

[129] Ibid.

[130] "Security clampdown in Russia," BBC News, World, Europe, September 15, 1999, http://news.bbc.co.uk/2/hi/europe/448005.stm (accessed January 21, 2012).

[131] Weir, "Fred Weir on treatment of Chechens."

[132] Ibid.

[133] Ibid.

[134] Ibid.

[135] Ibid.

[136] "Dagestan Incursions - August-September 1999," GlobalSecurity.org, http://www.globalsecurity.org/military/world/war/chechnya2-2.htm (accessed January 22, 2012).

[137] Gentleman, "Russia's shockwave of terror."

[138] "Chechnya," Encyclopedia Britannica Online, January 22, 2012, http://www.britannica.com/EBchecked/topic/108244/Chechnya (accessed January 22, 2012).

[139] "1997-1999: Peace, instability and internal unrest," The Telegraph, January 1, 2001, http://www.telegraph.co.uk/news/1399565/1997-1999-Peace-instability-and-internal-unrest.html (accessed April 12, 2012).

[140] Ibid.

[141] Michael Gordon, "Russia Persists With Its Vow to Destroy Rebels in Grozny," New York Times International, December 12, 1999, http://partners.nytimes.com/library/world/europe/121299russia-chechnya.html, (accessed April 15, 2012); Sarah Miller, "Russia vs. Chechnya: Round Two, The crisis moves west," FactMonster.com, October 8, 1999, http://www.factmonster.com/spot/chechnya1.html (accessed April 15, 2012).

[142] "U.S. Online Training Course for OSCE, including REACT: Module 7. Caucasus." United States Institute of Peace, http://react.usip.org/downloads/Module7.pdf (accessed April 15, 2012), 17.

[143] John Daly, "Domodevo and the Chechen Conflict" International Relations and Security Network, January 27, 2011, http://www.isn.ethz.ch/isn/Current-Affairs/ISN-Insights/Detail?lng =en&id=126470&contextid734=126470&contextid735=126466&tabid=126466(accessed April 15, 2012).

[144] "Phase Two – The Ground Campaign – October-November 1999," GlobalSecurity.org, http://www.globalsecurity.org/military/world/war/chechnya2-5.htm, (accessed January 22, 2012); Jim Nichol, *Chechnya Conflict: Recent Developments* (Washington, DC: U.S. Library of Congress, Congressional Research Service, May 3, 2000), 2.

[145] "Phase Two – The Ground Campaign – October-November 1999."

[146] Sergei Kovalev, "Putin's War," The New York Review of Books, January 13, 2000, http://www.nybooks.com/articles/archives/2000/feb/10/putins-war/?pagination=false (accessed April 19, 2012).

[147] "Chechnya," Encyclopedia Britannica Online, January 22, 2012, http://www.britannica.com/EBchecked/topic/108244/Chechnya (accessed January 22, 2012).

[148] Anup Shah, "Crisis in Chechnya," Global Issues, http://www.globalissues.org/article/100/ crisis-in-chechnya (accessed January 22, 2012).

[149] Ibid.

[150] "Chechnya," Encyclopedia Britannica Online, January 22, 2012, http://www.britannica.com/EBchecked/topic/108244/Chechnya (accessed January 22, 2012).

[151] Ibid.

[152] "First Chechnya War - 1994-1996," GlobalSecurity.org, Military, http://www.globalsecurity.org/military/world/war/chechnya1.htm (accessed April 19, 2012).

[153] Oleg Tsvetkov, "Ethnic Russians Flee the North Caucasus," *Migration, Regional Report, Russian Analytical digest Online*, No. 7 (October 3, 2006): 9, http://www.css.ethz.ch/ publications/pdfs/RAD-7.pdf (accessed 19 April, 2012).

[154] Charles King, "Crisis in the Caucasus: A New Look at Russia's Chechen Impasse," *Foreign Affairs* (March/April 2003), http://www.foreignaffairs.com/articles/58823/charles-king/crisis-in-the-caucasus-a-new-look-at-russia-s-chechen-impasse, (accessed April 19, 2012).

[155] "First Chechnya War - 1994-1996."

[156] Matt Bivens, "Russian Troops Are Selling Guns to Chechen Rebels: Warfare: Greed, not ideology, is apparently behind practice. It could well prolong the conflict in the breakaway region," Los Angeles Times, March 19, 1995, http://articles.latimes.com/1995-03-19/news/mn-44681_1_russian-army, (accessed 20 April 2012).

[157] "First Chechen War," New World Encyclopedia, http://www.newworldencyclopedia.org/ entry/First_Chechen_War (accessed April 20, 2012).

[158] The St. Petersburg Times, "Army Orders Clean Up of 'Cleansing'," April 2, 2002, http://www.sptimes.ru/archive/pdf/758.pdf, 1-2, (accessed January 22, 2012); Amelia Gentleman, "Civilian casualties of war in Chechnya," The Guardian, March 7, 2001, http://www.guardian.co.uk/world/2001/mar/07/worlddispatch.ameliagentleman (accessed April 20, 2012).

[159] James Meek, "The Russians are trying to take Grozny at any price," The Guardian, January 2, 1995, http://www.guardian.co.uk/world/1995/jan/03/chechnya.jamesmeek (accessed April 20, 2012).

[160] "Cries from the rubble," The Guardian, November 29, 1999, http://www.guardian.co.uk/world/1999/nov/30/chechnya.guardianleaders?INTCMP=ILCNETTXT3487 (accessed April 20, 2012).

[161] "Civilians Continue to Flee Violence in Chechnya," Doctors Without Borders, February 28, 2002, http://www.doctorswithoutborders.org/press/release.cfm?id=554 (accessed April 20, 2012); Ibid.

[162] Amelia Gentleman, "Chechen refugees face dire winter," The Guardian, October 26, 1999, http://www.guardian.co.uk/world/1999/oct/27/chechnya.ameliagentleman?INTCMP=ILCNETTXT3487, (accessed April 20, 2012); Jim Nichol, *Chechnya Conflict: Recent Developments* (Washington, DC: U.S. Library of Congress, Congressional Research Service, May 3, 2000), 6-8; "The Conflict in Chechnya," 22.

[163] Nichol, *"Chechnya Conflict: Recent Developments,"* 6-8.

[164] Reuven Paz, "Suicide Terrorist Operations in Chechnya: an escalation in the Islamist struggle," ICT, June 17, 2000, http://212.150.54.123/articles/articledet.cfm?articleid=113 (accessed January 21, 2012).

[165] "Chechnya," CBC News Online, July 10, 2006, http://www.cbc.ca/news/background/chechnya/ (accessed April 21, 2012).

[166] Nikolai Gorshkov, "Call to scrap Chechnya poll," BBC News, March 13, 2003, http://news.bbc.co.uk/2/hi/europe/2848893.stm (accessed April 21, 2012).

[167] Ibid.

[168] Gregory Feifer, "Chechnya: Russian Officials Say Chechen Referendum Broadly Approves Constitution," Radio Free Liberty Radio Europe, March 24, 2003, http://www.rferl.org/content/article/1102652.html (accessed April 21, 2012).

[169] Nikolai Gorshkov, "Putin urged to scrap Chechnya poll," BBC News, March 13, 2003, http://news.bbc.co.uk/2/hi/europe/2848893.stm (accessed February 8, 2012).

[170] Ibid.

[171] Gorshkov, "Putin urged to scrap Chechnya poll."

[172] Gregory Feifer, "Chechnya: Russian Officials Say Chechen Referendum Broadly Approves Constitution," Radio Free Liberty Radio Europe, March 24, 2003, http://www.rferl.org/content/article/1102652.html (accessed April 21, 2012).

[173] "Chechens vote on federation constitution," Associated Press, March 23, 2003, http://www.ctv.ca/CTVNews/World/20030323/chechens_constitution_20030323/ (accessed February 8, 2012); "Q & A: Chechen referendum," BBC News, March 21, 2003, http://news.bbc.co.uk/2/hi/europe/2873017.stm (accessed April 20, 2012).

[174] "Putin's man wins Chechen poll," BBC News, October 6, 2003, http://news.bbc.co.uk/2/hi/europe/3166586.stm (accessed February 8, 2012).

[175] Ibid.

[176] Ibid.

[177] Ibid.

[178] Ibid.

[179] Ibid.

[180] "Chechen president killed by bomb," BBC News, May 9, 2004, http://news.bbc.co.uk/2/hi/europe/3697715.stm (accessed February 9, 2012).

[181] Ibid.

[182] Charles Gurin, "Akhmad Kadyrov Is Assassinated," The Jamestown Foundation, May 9, 2004, http://www.jamestown.org/single/?no_cache=1&tx_ttnews%5Btt_news%5D=26479 (accessed April 21, 2012).

[183] "Obituary: Akhmad Kadyrov," BBC News, May 9, 2004, http://news.bbc.co.uk/go/pr/fr/-/2/hi/europe/3160962.stm (accessed February 9, 2012).

[184] Ibid.

[185] Ibid.

[186] Ibid.

[187] Gurin, "Akhmad Kadyrov Is Assassinated."

[188] Jim Nichol, *Bringing Peace to Chechnya? Assessments and Implications* (Washington, DC: U.S. Library of Congress, Congressional Research Service, CRS Report for Congress February 11, 2006), 7.

[189] "Regions and territories: Chechnya."

[190] "Timeline: Chechnya."

[191] "Obituary: Chechen Rebel Khattab," BBC News, World, Europe, April 26, 2002, http://news.bbc.co.uk/2/hi/europe/1952053.stm (accessed April 20, 2012).

[192] "Russia: Annotated Timeline of the Chechen Conflict," Radio Free Europe Radio Liberty, Russia, February 7, 2006, http://www.rferl.org/content/article/1065508.html (accessed April 21, 2012).

[193] "Aslan Maskhadov: An Appeal to the Russian President," Kommersant, Russia's Daily Online, February 9, 2005, http://www.kommersant.com/page.asp?id=545159 (accessed April 21, 2012).

[194] "Chechen leader Maskhadov killed," BBC News, March 8, 2005, http://news.bbc.co.uk/2/hi/europe/4330039.stm (accessed April 21, 2012).

[195] "Russia: Top Chechen Rebel Leader Killed," USA Today, World, June 17, 2006, http://www.usatoday.com/news/world/2006-06-17-chechen-leader_x.htm (accessed April 21, 2012).

[196] Liz Fuller, "News Profile: Who Is Doku Umarov?" Radio Free Europe Radio Liberty, April 1, 2012, http://www.rferl.org/content/News_Profile_Who_Is_Doku_Umarov/1999886.html (accessed April 21, 2012).

[197] "Chechen Rebel Chief Basayev Dies," BBC News, July 10, 2006, http://news.bbc.co.uk/2/hi/5165456.stm (accessed April 21, 2012).

[198] "The Conflict in Chechnya," 18.

[199] "Russia ends Chechnya operation," BBC News, April 16, 2009, http://news.bbc.co.uk/2/hi/europe/8001495.stm (accessed April 21, 2012).

[200] "North Caucasus: Guide to a volatile region."

[201] Gentleman, "Russia's shockwave of terror."

[202] Nabi Abdullaev, "Little Progress in Bomb Probe," The St. Petersburg Times, August 9, 2002, http://www.sptimes.ru/index.php?action_id=2&story_id=7818 (accessed January 22, 2012).

[203] Ibid.

[204] Ibid.

[205] Ibid.

[206] Ben Aris and Marcus Warren, "Eight killed in Moscow bomb blast," The Telegraph, August 9, 2000, http://www.telegraph.co.uk/news/worldnews/europe/russia/1352028/Eight-killed-in-Moscow-bomb-blast.html (accessed January 22, 2012).

[207] Ibid; "Moscow 'Terrorist' Bomb Kills 8," UPI, August 9, 2000, http://archive.newsmax.com/articles/?a=2000/8/8/171527 (accessed January 22, 2012).

[208] Ibid.

[209] Masha Gessen, "What really happened? Victims of the Moscow hostage crisis seek justice," usnews.com, Nation and World, January 27, 2003, http://www.usnews.com/ usnews/issue/030127/usnews/27hostage.htm.

[210] Rebecca Leung, "Terror in Moscow," cbsnews.com, February 11, 2009. http://www.cbsnews.com/stories/2003/10/24/60minutes/main579840.shtml (accessed April 21, 2012).

[211] Ibid.

[212] Elizabeth Anderson, "Hostage Taking in Moscow Condemned," Human Rights Watch, October 24, 2002, http//hrw.org/press/2002/10/russia1024.htm, 1.

[213] "Bloody end to Moscow hostage crisis," CBC News, October 29, 2002, http://www.cbc.ca/news/world/story/2002/10/26/Moscow_theatre021026.html (accessed April 21, 2012).

[214] "How special forces ended siege," BBC News, October 29, 2002, http://news.bbc.co.uk/2/hi/europe/2363601.stm, 1-6 (accessed February 9, 2012).

[215] Ibid.

[216] Ibid.

[217] Ibid.

[218] Ibid.

[219] "Independent Commission of Inquiry Must Investigate Raid on Moscow Theater: Inadequate Preparation for Consequences of Gas Violates Obligation to Protect Life," Human Rights Watch. New York, October 30, 2002, 1-2.

[220] Gessen, "What really happened?"

[221] "Independent Commission of Inquiry Must Investigate Raid on Moscow Theater: Inadequate Preparation for Consequences of Gas Violates Obligation to Protect Life," 1-2.

[222] Ibid; "How special forces ended siege," 1-6.

[223] Lagnado, Alice, "Chechens feel the heat as racial backlash begins," Johnson's Russia List, October 29, 2002, http://www.cdi.org/russia/johnson/6519-10.cfm (accessed February 9, 2012).

[224] Ibid.

[225] Gregory Feifer, "Russia: Moscow's Vow To Fight Terrorism Criticized Amid Theater-Raid Fallout," Radio Free Europe Radio Liberty, October 30, 2002, http://www.rferl.org/content/ article/1101227.html (accessed February 9, 2012).

[226] Ibid.

[227] Ibid.

[228] Ibid.

[229] "Moscow metro blast kills 39: Putin blames Chechen rebel leader," The Guardian, guardian.co.uk, February 6, 2004, http://www.guardian.co.uk/world/2004/feb/06/russia?INTCMP=ILCNETTXT3487 (accessed February 9, 2012).

[230] "Many dead in Moscow metro blast," BBC News, February 6, 2004, http://news.bbc.co.uk/2/hi/europe/3464545.stm (accessed April 21, 2012).

[231] Ibid.

[232] Ibid.

[233] "Moscow metro hit by deadly suicide bombings," BBC News, March 29, 2010, http://news.bbc.co.uk/2/hi/europe/8592190.stm (accessed April 21, 2012).

[234] "Second Moscow bomber identified," BBC News, March 6, 2010, http://news.bbc.co.uk/go/pr/fr/-/2/hi/europe/8604535.stm (accessed April 21, 2012).

[235] "Moscow metro hit by deadly suicide bombings."

[236] "Teenage widow was Moscow bomber," BBC News, http://news.bbc.co.uk/2/hi/europe/8600563.stm, April 2, 2010 (accessed April 21, 2012).

[237] "Chechen rebel claims Metro blasts," BBC News, March 31, 2010, http://news.bbc.co.uk/2/hi/europe/8597792.stm (accessed April 21, 2012).

[238] "Suicide bomber kills 35 at Russia's biggest airport," Reuters, January 24, 2011, http://www.reuters.com/article/2011/01/24/us-russia-blast-airport-idUSTRE70N2TQ20110124 (accessed April 21, 2012).

[239] Ibid.

[240] Tom Parfitt, "Domodedovo bomb shows security was in state of anarchy, says Medvedev," The Guardian, January 25, 2011, http://www.guardian.co.uk/world/2011/jan/25/domodedovo-bomb-failure-kremlin (accessed April 21, 2012).

[241] Ibid.

[242] Ibid.

[243] Ivan Sekretarev, "Putin vows retribution for deadly bomb attack," USA Today, January 25, 2011, http://www.usatoday.com/news/world/2011-01-25-russia-airport-bombing_N.htm (accessed February 11, 2012).

[244] Ibid.

[245] Ibid.

[246] Ibid.

[247] Ibid.

[248] Ibid.

[249] Menon, "Russia's hot spot."

[250] "Medvedev Creates New North Caucasus Federal District," Radio Free Europe Radio Liberty, Caucasus Report, January 20, 2010, http://www.rferl.org/content/Medvedev_Creates_New_North_Caucasus_Federal_District/1934705.html (accessed March 17, 2012).

[251] Ibid.

[252] Ibid.

[253] Ibid.

[254] Ibid.

[255] Ibid.

[256] Ibid.

[257] Preeti Bhattacharji, "Chechen Terrorism (Russia, Chechnya, Separatist)," Council on Foreign Relations, Backgrounder, April 8, 2010, http://www.cfr.org/terrorism/chechen-terrorism-russia-chechnya-separatist/p9181 (accessed February 11, 2012).

[258] Annie Atura, "Martyrdom Usurped: Chechnya's Black Widows," Broad Recognition, April 6, 2010, http://broadrecognition.com/politics/martyrdom-usurped-chechnyas-black-widows/ (accessed February 11, 2012).

[259] Menon, "Russia's hot spot."

[260] "Chechen leader Maskhadov killed."

[261] Gordon, "Russia Persists With Its Vow to Destroy Rebels in Grozny."

[262] Cornell, "The War in Chechnya: A Regional Time Bomb," Global Dialogue Online, Volume 7, Number 3-4, (Summer/Autumn 2005-The Volatile Caucasus). http://www.worlddialogue.org/content.php?id=349, (accessed April 21, 2012).

[263] Ibid.

[264] Philpot, "The North Caucasus: Russian Roulette on Europe's Borders," 93.

[265] "North Caucasus: Guide to a volatile region."

[266] Ibid.

[267] Kathy Lally, "In Russia's Dagestan, Salafi Muslims clash with government authorities," September 5, 2011, http://www.washingtonpost.com/world/in-russias-dagestan-salafi-muslims-clash-with-government-authorities/2011/07/15/gIQAeBo82J_story.html (accessed February 12, 2012).

[268] "North Caucasus: Guide to a volatile region."

[269] "Lukoil plans to invest in North Caucasus," Vestnik Kavkaza, April 28, 2011, http://vestnikkavkaza.net/news/economy/13336.html (accessed March 18, 2012).

[270] Lally, "In Russia's Dagestan, Salafi Muslims clash with government authorities,"

[271] Ibid.

[272] Ibid.

[273] Ibid.

[274] Ibid.

[275] Ibid.

[276] Ibid.

[277] Ibid.

[278] Ibid.

[279] Ibid.

[280] Ibid.

[281] Ibid.

[282] "Profile: Chechen rebel leader Doku Umarov," BBC News Europe, March 30, 2011, http://www.bbc.co.uk/news/world-europe-12269155 (accessed March 28, 2012).

[283] Ibid.

[284] Lally, "In Russia's Dagestan, Salafi Muslims clash with government authorities."

[285] "North Caucasus: Guide to a volatile region."

[286] Ibid.

[287] Ibid.

[288] Claire Bigg, "Five Years After Nazran, Ingushetia Still Plagued By Militant Violence," Radio Free Europe Radio Liberty, June 19, 2009, http://www.rferl.org/content/

Five_Years_After_Nazran_Ingushetia_Still_Plagued_By_Militant_Violence/1758428.html (accessed March 18, 2012).

[289] Ibid.

[290] Ibid.

[291] "North Caucasus: Guide to a volatile region."

[292] Ibid.

[293] Ibid.

[294] Ibid.

[295] Grigory Shedov and Alexy Malashenko, "North Caucasus: Results of 2010," Carnegie Endowment For International Peace, March 15, 2011, http://carnegieendowment.org/ 2011/03/15/north%2Dcaucasus%2Dresults%2Dof%2D2010/41rj (accessed March 18, 2012).

[296] Ibid.

[297] Ibid.

[298] Ibid.

[299] "North Caucasus: Guide to a volatile region."

[300] Ibid.

[301] "Beslan, North Ossetia," GlobalSecurity.org, Military, http://www.globalsecurity.org/ military/world/war/chechnya-beslan.htm (accessed April 21, 2012).

[302] Ibid.

[303] Ibid.

[304] Ibid.

[305] "Russians mourn car bomb victims," The Guardian, September 10, 2010, http://www.guardian.co.uk/world/2010/sep/10/russians-mourn-car-bomb-victims (accessed April 21, 2012).

[306] "North Caucasus: Guide to a volatile region."

[307] Ibid.

[308] Ibid.

[309] Ibid.

[310] "Kabardino-Balkaria profile," BBC News, November 22, 2011, http://news.bbc.co.uk/2/hi/europe/country_profiles/4338292.stm (accessed April 21, 2012).

[311] Shedov and Alexy Malashenko, "North Caucasus: Results of 2010."

[312] "North Caucasus: Guide to a volatile region."

[313] Ibid.

[314] "Regions and territories: Karachay-Cherkessia," BBC News, November 22, 2011, http://news.bbc.co.uk/go/pr/fr/-/2/hi/europe/country_profiles/5381570.stm (accessed March 19, 2012.

[315] "Stavropol Territory," Background Places, Russia Profile.org, 2011, http://russiaprofile.org/bg_places/resources_territory_districts_stavropol.html (accessed March 19, 2012).

[316] Andrei Smirnov, "Fighting Erupts Between Nogai Rebels and Russian Authorities," The Jamestown Foundation, Eurasia Daily Monitor Volume: 3 Issue: 33, February 16, 2006, http://www.jamestown.org/programs/edm/single/?tx_ttnews%5Btt_news%5D=31396&tx_ttnews%5BbackPid%5D=177&no_cache=1 (accessed March 19, 2012).

[317] Shedov and Alexy Malashenko, "North Caucasus: Results of 2010."

[318] Ibid.

[319] Smirnov, "Fighting Erupts Between Nogai Rebels and Russian Authorities."

[320] Ibid.

[321] Ibid.

[322] Ibid.

[323] Ibid.

[324] Natalya Krainova, "Suicide Bombers Strike in Caucasus," The Moscow Times, Feb. 16, 2011, http://www.cdi.org/russia/johnson/russia-terrorist-attack-caucasus-feb-375.cfm (accessed March 19, 2012).

[325] Ibid.

[326] Ibid.

[327] Ibid.

[328] Gordon Hahn, "Russia's Thaw - - Through The North Caucasus Prism," Russia: Other Points of View, August 12, 2010, http://www.typepad.com/services/trackback/6a00e00982df3e88330133f307e3ac970b (accessed March 18, 2012).

[329] "North Caucasus: Guide to a volatile region."

[330] "OGPSS - Oil production from the North Caucasus."

[331] Ibid.

[332] "Lukoil plans to invest in North Caucasus," Vestnik Kavkaza.

[333] Shirin Akiner, "Politics of Energy in the Caspian Sea Region," 15.

[334] Ibid., 15.

[335] Ibid., 15.

[336] Ibid., 12.

[337] Ibid., 12.

[338] Ibid., 12.

[339] Ibid., 12.

[340] "Prime Minister Putin promised development of a oil center project in Chechnya," Neftegaz.ru, News, Russia, July 7, 2010, http://neftegaz.ru/en/news/view/95732 (accessed March 18, 2012).

[341] Ibid.

[342] "Russia, Country Analysis Brief," U.S. Energy Information Administration, July 14, 2010, http://205.254.135.7/countries/country-data.cfm?fips=RS&trk=c (accessed March 18, 2012).

[343] Ioannis Vichos and Sotirios Karampampas, "The security situation in North Caucasus and the energy factor."

[344] "Sochi 2014," Olympic.org, Official Website of the Olympic Movement, http://www.olympic.org/sochi-2014-winter-olympics (accessed March 18, 2012).

[345] "Sochi: A Warm Vacation All Year," Official Administration Site of the Resort City of Sochi, http://www.eng.sochiru.ru/ (accessed March 18, 2012).

[346] "Prime Minister Putin promised development of a oil center project in Chechnya."

[347] Ibid.

[348] Ibid.

[349] Ibid.

[350] Levy, "Russia Faces 3-Year Race to Secure Site of Olympics."

[351] Hahn, "Russia's Thaw - - Through The North Caucasus Prism."

[352] Ibid.

[353] Ibid.

[354] Ibid.

[355] Ibid.

[356] Ibid.

[357] Philpot, "The North Caucasus: Russian Roulette on Europe's Borders," 94.

[358] Andrew Kuchins, Matthew Malarkey, Sergei Markedonov, "The North Caucasus, Russia's Volatile Frontier," Center for Strategic and International Studies, March 2011, http://csis.org/event/north-caucasus-russias-volatile-frontier (accessed April 21, 2012).

[359] Ibid.

[360] Ibid., 12.

[361] Ibid.

[362] "OGPSS - Oil production from the North Caucasus."

[363] Hahn, "Russia's Thaw - - Through The North Caucasus Prism."

[364] "Prime Minister Putin promised development of a oil center project in Chechnya."

[365] Ibid.

[366] Ibid.

[367] Philpot, "The North Caucasus: Russian Roulette on Europe's Borders," 94.

[368] "Russia: Putin calls for 'comprehensive' fight against terrorism," FBIS, ITAR-TASS, Moscow, October 2, 2001, in Open Source Center (accessed January 27, 2012).

[369] "Medvedev Creates New North Caucasus Federal District."

www.ingramcontent.com/pod-product-compliance
Lightning Source LLC
Chambersburg PA
CBHW080535290526
45790CB00006B/2421